The Johannine Gospel in Gnostic Exegesis

Society of Biblical Literature
Monograph Series 17

Robert A. Kraft, Editor (1967-72)
Leander Keck, Editor (1973-)

Published for the
Society of Biblical Literature

Elaine H. Pagels

THE JOHANNINE GOSPEL
IN GNOSTIC EXEGESIS
Heracleon's Commentary on John

Scholars Press
Atlanta, Georgia

THE JOHANNINE GOSPEL
IN GNOSTIC EXEGESIS

by

Elaine H. Pagels

Library of Congress Cataloging in Publication Data

Pagels, Elaine H., 1943-
 The Johannine Gospel in Gnostic exegesis : Heracleon's commentary
on John / by Elaine H. Pagels.
  p. cm. -- (Monograph series / Society of Biblical Literature
: no. 17)
  Reprint. Originally published: Nashville : Abingdon Press, 1973.
  Includes bibliographical references and indexes.
  ISBN 1-55540-334-4 (alk. paper)
  1. Bible. N.T. John--Criticism, interpretation, etc.--History-
-Early church, ca. 30-600. 2. Gnosticism. 3. Heracleon, the
Gnostic. 4. Valentinians. I. Title. II. Series: Monograph series
(Society of Biblical Literature) : no. 17.
BS2615.2.P24 1989
226'.506'0882999--dc19   89-6090
                                                       CIP

Printed in the United States of America
on acid-free paper

Acknowledgments

In the preparation of the present work I have received guidance from numerous colleagues, teachers, and friends to whom I am indebted for assistance in many ways. I am especially indebted to Helmut Koester of Harvard University, who advised me in producing the dissertation which underlies the present work; to Robert Kraft of the University of Pennsylvania, who has offered great assistance in preparing the manuscript; and to Theodore H. Gaster of Barnard College and Columbia University, whose continual encouragement and scholarly advice have proven invaluable.

Contents

Abbreviations

AH
Adversus Haereses, Irenaeus, ed. W. W. Harvey (Cambridge, 1857); text divisions follow those of R. Massuet, in Migne, *Patrologia Graeca* 7 (1857). These are also noted in Harvey's margins.

1 Apoc Jas
I Apocalypse Jacobi, in: *Koptische-Gnostische Apokalypsen aus Codex V von Nag Hammadi,* ed. A. Böhlig and P. Labib (Halle, 1963), pp. 34.10–54.9.

Apol
Apologia prima pro Christianis, Justin Martyr, in: *Justinus, Opera Omnia,* ed. J. C. Otto (Jena, 3rd ed., 1876).

CJ
Commentarium in Johannis, Origen, ed. E. Preuschen GCS 4 (Leipzig, 1903).

CR
Le Commentaire d'Origène sur Rom III.5–V.7 d'après les Extraits du Pap. No. 88748 du Musée de Caire et les Frag. de la Philoc. et du Vat. Gr. 762, ed. J. Scherer, in: Inst. Fr. d'Arch. Orient., Bibl. d'Etude, T. 27 (Cairo, 1957).

Ep
Epistola ad Floram, Ptolemy, ed., transl. and intro. by G. Quispel, in: Sources Chrétiennes 24 (1949).

Ev Phil
Das Evangelium nach Philippos, Coptic text ed. and transl. W. C. Till, Patristische Texte und Studien 2 (Berlin, 1963). See also English translation by R. McL. Wilson, *The Gospel of Philip* (London, 1962).

9

Ev Thom *Evangelium Thomae,* Coptic text ed. and transl. by A. Guillaumont, H.-C. Puech, G. Quispel, W. Till, Yassah 'Abd al Masiḥ (Leiden, 1959).

Ev Ver *Evangelium Veritatis,* Coptic text ed. and transl. M. Malinine, H.-C. Puech, G. Quispel (Zurich, 1956) : *Evangelium Veritatis (Supplementum)*, Coptic text ed. and transl. M. Malinine, H. C. Puech, G. Quispel, W. C. Till (Zurich, 1961).

Exc *The Excerpta ex Theodoto of Clement of Alexandria,* ed., transl., and intro. by R. P. Casey (London, 1934).

GCS *Die griechischen christlichen Schriftsteller der ersten Jahrhunderte.*

Pan *Panarion,* Epiphanius, ed. K. Holl
    1 Ancoratus and Panarion, Haer. 1-33, GCS 25 (1915)
    2 Panarion Haer. 34-64, GCS 31 (1922)
    3 Panarion Haer. 65-80; De Fide, GCS 37 (1933).

Prin *De Principiis,* Origen, ed. P. Koetschau, GCS 5 (1913).

Ref *Refutatio Omnium Haeresium,* Hippolytus, in: *Opera* 3, ed. P. Wendland, GCS 26 (1916).

Strom *Stromata,* Clement of Alexandria, ed. O. Stahlin, GCS 12, 15, 17, 39 (1906-1939).

Introduction

Those diverse interpreters of the Christian message whom Irenaeus calls "gnostics" (whatever differences they may have had among themselves) agree on one point: that the majority of their Christian contemporaries misinterpret the revelation in Christ. Gnostic critics claim that the basic error of "the many" involves their preoccupation with the historical reality of Jesus.

Who are "the many" whom these gnostics attack? Can we assume that they mean what Clement and Origen mean when they use the term —the mass of uneducated Christians? S. Laeuchli recently has argued that the gnostic movement originated as the reaction of an educated minority to the emerging phenomenon of "popular Christianity." [1] Certainly men like Valentinus, Basilides, Marcus, Ptolemy, Heracleon, and Theodotus distinguish themselves as skilled and articulate intellectuals among the majority of second-century Christians. But Irenaeus points out that there are highly educated and gifted theologians among "the churches" as well. Yet none of these use their theological reflection to change the basic "postulate" (*hypothesis*) of the faith itself—as he claims the gnostics do (AH 1.10.2-3).

The gnostic theologians, for their part, deny that they have separated

[1] S. Laeuchli, from a talk given in October, 1971, at the New York Patristics Seminar.

11

themselves from the common "postulate." Hippolytus admits that what he calls the "blasphemy against Christ" of the Peratae had "always gone unnoticed" in Christian circles until he himself singled them out for attack (Ref 5.12). Irenaeus acknowledges that the Valentinians themselves say they "accept the common postulate"; they identify themselves to this extent with the Christian majority. But he adds that in their alleged profession of the faith they interpret it "idiosyncratically": for them it means something quite different from what it means for Irenaeus—himself a learned theologian.

Irenaeus perceives that the gnostics are not simply reacting against naïvely "popular" versions of Christian teaching. He sees that they are challenging nothing less than the fundamental theological standpoint —not only of the actual numerical majority, but also of its most educated and articulate spokesmen, including Justin, Irenaeus himself, Tertullian, and Hippolytus.

The Jesus of history and the gnostic Christ

What is this fundamental "postulate" that they challenge? Above all it is the claim that the man Jesus who lived "in the flesh" is "Christ": that the revelation of God has been given in and through the actual events of his coming.

Justin, for example, draws a sharp contrast between pagan religious myths and the proclamation of Christ. He admits that "in saying that the logos is born for us without sexual union, as Jesus Christ our teacher, and that he was crucified and died, and after rising again ascended into heaven, we introduce nothing new" beyond what pagans claim of the "so-called sons of Zeus" (Apol 21). The crucial difference is that the myths are false, poetic fictions, but the Christian claim is actually true: "Jesus Christ alone really *was* born as the son of God" (Apol 23). Justin adds that no one could be expected to believe this without proof (as children are expected to believe the myths). To demonstrate that "we do not, like those who tell the mythical stories about the so-called sons of Zeus, merely talk, without having proof," he claims that "we have found testimonies proclaimed about him before he came . . . and see that these things have happened" (Apol 53).

Justin refers for his proof to the Christian "gospels"—which he calls the apostles' "memoirs." These offer eyewitness accounts that the events prophesied actually have occurred. For Justin, the events themselves

—and not the evangelistic and apostolic writings that attest them—
are the primary means of revelation. The *significance* of the "gospels"
is that they provide the necessary evidence for the Christian claim. The
validity of their witness is confirmed, in turn, by the exact correlation
of the events they recount with ancient prophecies.

Irenaeus, like Justin, insists that "the church" stands on the con-
viction that "God was made man" (AH 3.21.1), specifically the man
Jesus of Nazareth, who was born "about the forty-first year of Augustus'
reign" (3.21.2), lived, suffered, and died "in the flesh," and was raised
from the dead according to prophecy. These stand as the "first principles of the gospel" (AH 3.11.6; apparently Irenaeus uses the term
"gospel," as von Campenhausen points out, in its early, Pauline sense[2]).
Irenaeus declares that the prophetic "scriptures" "assist" the preaching
of the gospel by having given divinely inspired predictions in advance.
The four "gospel" writings he accepts as valid documents attest the
fulfillment of these predictions in the events of Christ's coming.

The gnostics challenge these very "first principles." Gnostic theologians do not necessarily *deny* that the events proclaimed of Jesus
have occurred in history. What they deny is that the actuality of these
events matters *theologically*. Heracleon claims, for example, that those
who insist that Jesus, a man who lived "in the flesh," is "Christ" fail
to distinguish between literal and symbolic truth. Those who write
accounts of the revelation as alleged biographies of "Jesus of Nazareth"
—or even of Jesus as messiah—focus on mere historical "externals"
and miss the inner truth they signify.

Significance of "gospels" in gnostic exegesis

Irenaeus' account of the Valentinian theory of revelation (AH
4.19.2) indicates that Heracleon here speaks for Valentinian tradition
in general. But the Valentinians never suggest that their Christian
contemporaries in the second century have originated this "error."
They trace its course through the "canonical" gospels to the circle of
the disciples themselves. They point out how often Christ rebukes
the disciples for taking his symbolic statements literally (cf AH
3.12.1 f; CJ 13.35). They see Peter as, perhaps, the worst offender, the
most persistent in this attitude of stubborn literal-mindedness (AH
3.12.9). The Valentinians express dismay, but no surprise, at seeing the

[2] H. F. von Campenhausen, *Die Entstehung der christlichen Bibel* (Tübingen,
1968), 213.

majority of contemporary Christians (especially those who are beginning to claim an "apostolic foundation" for their faith) emulating the disciples' literalism as well as their faith.

Heracleon goes on to say that those who take the events concerning Jesus "literally"—as if the events *themselves* were revelation—have fallen into "flesh and error" (CJ 13.19). Their error consists in mistaking literal, historical *data* for spiritual truth. They fail to recognize these events as "images." To recognize their true meaning, one must come to see that these events do not in themselves *effect* redemption. Rather, they serve to symbolize the process of redemption that occurs within those who perceive their inner meaning.

Gnostic teachers attempt to formulate Christian theology in terms they consider more theologically significant than through the approach to the "earthly Jesus" whose presence dominates the synoptics. Some— like Valentinus himself—put forth original writings such as those "gospels," revelation discourses, treatises, hymns, and prayers familiar to us as "New Testament apocrypha." Diverse as these are in genre and theological viewpoint,[3] they attempt in common to interpret the revelation of Christ in terms of its inner, symbolic meaning.

Certain other gnostic theologians, instead of producing original "gospels," apply themselves to exegete "spiritually" those gospels already familiar to the majority of Christians—those which even Irenaeus admits accord with the "canon" of the church's faith (cf AH 3.9.1–11.9). These theologians intend their "spiritual exegesis" to demonstrate the "error" of literal reading, and to raise the reader's consciousness to the level of symbolic interpretation.

Gnostic approaches to the "gospels," then, differ radically from those of their theological opponents. They tend to dismiss as "literalism" the apologists' view of the gospels. Gnostic theologians claim that those apparently simple gospel narratives are actually allegories—which, read "spiritually," disclose in symbolic language the process of inner redemption. They recognized that to explicate the symbolic truths hidden in scripture would require nothing less than to develop a new hermeneutical method—and this is precisely what they have done. Hippolytus relates as clear evidence of their heterodoxy that the Naassenes and the Peratae have developed a "new hermeneutical dis-

---

[3] H. Koester, "One Jesus and Four Primitive Gospels," *Harvard Theological Review* 61 (1968), 205 f. Most of the new apocryphal material is now available in E. Hennecke and W. Schneemelcher, *New Testament Apocrypha* 1–2, Eng. transl. and ed. by R. McL. Wilson (Philadelphia, 1963-65), from: Neutestamentliche Apokryphen 1–2 (Tübingen, 1959-64).

cipline." Although they apply this hermeneutical discipline to both the Jewish scriptures and the Christian gospels, the Naassenes do not share Hippolytus' concern to correlate events and "types" in the Jewish scriptures with events recounted in the gospels. Instead they approach both Jewish and Christian writings as they approach classical poetry—as a corpus of symbolically written sacred literature.

Such sacred writings must, they assume, be directed toward the profoundest questions of existence: they must reveal the nature of "all things." Yet one could not expect to understand the significance of such writings from a naïve and uninstructed reading of them. Whoever would interpret them must first receive a preliminary theological instruction (which they claim to offer)—an "initiation into gnosis." Summarized, their initiatory doctrine states that "whoever says that all things are derived from one (principle) is deceived; whoever says (they are derived) from three, speaks truth, and gives the exposition concerning the whole" (Ref 5.8.1.). By means of this principle the Naassenes claim to find "scriptural proof" for their teachings. They demonstrate their doctrine of the primal Anthropos from Isa 53.8, as from other passages from Jewish and Christian writings. In Hippolytus' discussion of their exegesis, references to John and Matthew occur frequently; they also cite Luke, Mark, and the Pauline letters.

This theological initiation enables them to interpret not only the gospels (including "apocrypha," Ref 5.7.9;5.7.20) but whatever writings express (as they believe Jesus' sayings do) knowledge of the "mysteries" of human existence. They explain that these mysteries are the utterance of the primal Anthropos, the archetype of humanity. Knowledge of these mysteries emerges universally in human experience: the initiated find allusions to them in the poetry of Anacreon and Homer and in the sacraments of Phyrgia and Eleusis, as well as in the sayings of Jesus.

The Naassenes are denying what Justin, Irenaeus, and Hippolytus regard as the unique validity of the revelation in Christ. They reject the "earthly Jesus" along with the "simple" reading of the gospels— that is, the narrative level which recounts his life, death, and resurrection—just as they would reject a literal reading of the Attis myth. Since truth consists in a potentially universal process of coming to "know" the spiritual meaning of existence, they claim that only those who have been initiated and have "become truly gnostics" are able to perceive the "great and ineffable mystery" (Ref 5.8.27) underlying the words of a sacred text. The literal level of *any* text, then, including that of the gospels, offers only the outward manifestation of inner meaning; it contains the metaphorical form of the ineffable truth.

Historical data and theological insight: two points of view

Of course there are self-professed "ecclesiastical" Christians—notably such Alexandrians as Clement and Origen—who *also* apprehend the "scriptures" as "religious literature" and seek to expound its "hidden" symbolic meaning. But these Christians declare that they intend to carry out the theological task Irenaeus commends—to develop theological reflection on the basis of the "common postulate" of the church's faith. Unlike the Valentinians, they never repudiate the "logos made flesh" or the "literal level" of the gospel accounts that narrate the actual events of the incarnation. Origen states, for example, at the start of his treatise on "first principles" (1.1-4) and of his commentary on John (CJ 1.5-6) that these stand as the necessary foundation for all his theological reflection. Although he is not content to *remain* on the level of apprehending Christ through the "human Jesus" and through the literal level of the text, he insists that these must serve as the basic postulate from which theological insight may develop. His Valentinian opponents, on the contrary, claim that such *data* tend to obstruct the process of attaining such insight. Far from serving as the necessary, primary postulate for attaining gnosis, they prove to be a source of "ignorance and error."

Exegesis of John in gnostic circles

Given their theory of revelation, it is no wonder that gnostic theologians are the first known authors to have produced exegetical commentaries on the "evangelistic and apostolic sayings" (CJ Frag 16). The earliest known example of these comes from the Valentinian theologian Heracleon (*ca.*160-180) as his commentary on the Johannine gospel. This gospel early became the focus of hermeneutical controversy. Heracleon's contemporary Ptolemy also offers systematic exegesis of the Johannine prologue (AH 1.8.5). Even earlier, apparently, the Naassenes and Peratae referred to the fourth gospel to the virtual exclusion of the synoptics (Ref 5-7). The Valentinians used it so extensively that Irenaeus says that to refute their teaching he has been compelled to refute their false exegesis of John (AH 3.11.7).

This study is intended to investigate gnostic, especially Valentinian, exegesis of the Johannine gospel. How did gnostic exegetes actually interpret it? Is their exegesis as hopelessly "arbitrary" and "contrived" as Irenaeus, Clement, and Origen allege (with concurrence from several recent scholars[4]) ? Does it reflect any systematic methodology? Most important, what theological presuppositions underlie their hermeneutical practice, and what theological issues are at stake in the controversy over Johannine exegesis?

The method for this investigation is to examine the known fragments of gnostic Johannine exegesis, and to analyze their interrelation as well as their relation to the Johannine exegesis of Irenaeus, Clement, and Origen. Valentinian exegeses of John offer the most extensive source material, especially as reflected in the fragments of Heracleon's commentary. These fragments provide the main focus for this study.

How representative is Heracleon?

Such a method raises a question: On the basis of Heracleon's exegesis, is it legitimate to make inferences about "gnostic," or even Valentinian, theology and hermeneutics in general? De Faye suggests that neither Ptolemy nor Heracleon can be taken as representing the type of theology that Irenaeus and Hippolytus characterize as "Valentinian." He suggests that Ptolemy and Heracleon reflect instead a "strictly monotheistic" development within Valentinian tradition; that they deliberately omit from their theology the "mythopoetic" formulations of Valentinus and his earlier followers.[5] Brooke[6] and von Loewenich[7] agree that Heracleon's exegetical insight into the fourth gospel has "compelled" him to break with the "usual dogmatic-gnostic interpretation" of John. Sanders adds that Heracleon's Valentinianism has been "profoundly modified by his study of the fourth gospel." [8] The conclusions of Brooke, von Loewenich, and Sanders rest, I believe, on what these scholars assume is the "true" interpretation of John. The present study should demonstrate that Heracleon does not share these assumptions: instead they form the central issue of the hermeneutical controversy.

---

[4] Cf. W. von Loewenich, *Das Johannes-Verständnis im zweiten Jahrhundert* (Giessen, 1932) , 76.

[5] E. de Faye, *Gnostiques et Gnosticisme* (Paris, 1913) , 108.

[6] A. E. Brooke, *The Fragments of Heracleon*, Texts and Studies I.4 (Cambridge, 1891) , 50.

[7] *Johannes-Verständnis*, 84.

[8] J. N. Sanders, *The Fourth Gospel in the Early Church* (Cambridge, 1943) , 64.

17

But how are we to explain the fact that Heracleon never refers explicitly to (for example) the myth of the pleromic aions? Origen says that Heracleon presupposes it—but his remarks could reveal only his misinformation or his intention to discredit Heracleon's theology. Furthermore, the fragments of Valentinus, Ptolemy's Letter to Flora, and the (presumably Valentinian) Gospel of Truth *also* omit reference to the pleromic myth. Could these (together with Heracleon's exegesis) represent a type of Valentinian theology *not* concerned with such mythology? Could they represent not a more "highly developed" Valentinianism, but, on the contrary, an earlier and more original version? In this case the pleromic myth and the myth of Sophia's fall might have been incorporated later (perhaps from other sources) into Valentinian theology. This could explain how Ptolemy's Letter to Flora proves to be so consistent with Heracleon's exegesis. Yet this hypothesis cannot withstand a full examination of the evidence from Ptolemy and Heracleon. For if it is true (as I believe) that Ptolemy *also* has written the Johannine exegesis presented in AH 1.8.5, his theology *does* include specific description of the pleromic creation of aions. How can the discrepancy between his Johannine exegesis and his Letter be resolved? I would suggest that this discrepancy offers a clear example of how a Valentinian theologian could present a clear, consistent, and intentionally *exoteric* or publically oriented exposition of his theology for non-initiates (like Flora), while reserving his *esoteric* theology (including the pleromic myth) for initiates (cf AH 1.8.5). By analogy, I suggest that Heracleon intends his Johannine exegesis to be read by non-initiates (hence its agreement with Ptolemy's Letter).

Yet even Heracleon refers, in his exegesis, to a pre-cosmic myth. He mentions that the "son of man beyond the *topos*" effects the pre-cosmic "sowing of the seed" which the "son of man" in the *cosmos* reaps (CJ 13.49). In another passage he states that the logos provides pneumatics with their primary "genesis" that prepares their "formation" in the cosmos (CJ 2.21). Such references indicate that Heracleon, like Ptolemy, does regard the pre-cosmic myth as the presupposition of his theological exposition. Furthermore, his exegesis of Jn 4 follows the structure of the Sophia myth in such detail that Sagnard concludes that the Samaritan must be an image of Sophia.[9] But Heracleon omits any mention of so obvious an inference. I believe that this omission is certainly deliberate. These observations, together with Ptolemy's ex-

[9] F. Sagnard, *La Gnose valentinienne et le témoignage de Saint Irénée* (Paris, 1947), 502.

ample, lead me to conclude that Heracleon, like Ptolemy, does presuppose the mythopoetic theology that Irenaeus, Hippolytus, and Origen ascribe to him. Yet these observations also indicate that both Ptolemy and Heracleon consciously discriminate between their exoteric teaching (available to outsiders) and their esoteric teaching (which includes the pleromic and kenomic mythology) reserved for initiates. The Valentinians claim Christ as their example of a teacher who adapts his teaching to the capacity of his audience (cf AH 3.5.1). As a cardinal principle of gnostic teaching, it earns Irenaeus' vehement censure, for he perceives that this same epistemological principle underlies Valentinian christological and soteriological theology as well as Valentinian hermeneutical practice.

1. Jn 1.1-4 in Gnostic Exegesis

Given their theory of revelation, how do gnostic theologians actually apply it to the text of the Johannine gospel? Comparative analysis of gnostic exegesis of Jn 1.3 from Naassene, Peratae, and Valentinian sources offers a starting point for investigating this question.

Naassene exegesis

The Naassenes, reading that "all things were made through him" (Jn 1.3), reject the "simple reading" which would suggest that the passage refers to the demiurge "through whom" all things were created. Such a reading would interpret the verse in terms of a "single" and therefore "deceptive" principle. With this they reject the monism of ordinary Christians who worship the demiurge as the only creator. This demiurge the Naassenes call the "fourth God." They consider him to be the creator of materiality alone (Ref 5.7.31). The demiurge, then, falls below the three metaphysical principles which their theology presupposes: the passage cannot, therefore, refer to him. To whom, then, does it refer?

Invoking their "threefold principle" (see above, p. 15), they go on to claim that Jn 1.3 supports their doctrine that "all things" derive from the three principles of being in the primal anthropos (Ref 5.8.5).

"The first principle (*archē*) of all things" is that of the "blessed nature (*physis*) of the blessed anthropos from above, Adam" (Ref 5.8.2). From him the "spiritual" (*pneumatikoi*) derive, and to him they return (Ref 5.8.44). The name they apply to him, Caulacau, like the names of the other two anthropological principles, is taken from an allegorical interpretation of Isa 28.10 (Ref 5.8.4).[1] Opposite to Caulacau in their anthropological trinity is the "mortal and perishable" anthropos, Saulasau. The median principle between them, called Zeesar, represents the anthropos in a state of alienation from his divine origin, presently enslaved to the "powers" of materiality, yet destined to escape their domination and return to his divine origin. "The ignorant," not perceiving his inner, divine nature, call him "tribodied Geryon," "as if he flowed from earth" (a name they trace etymologically to the Greek verb (*h*)*rein*, to flow, and *gē*, earth). This divine archetypal anthropos, they explain, is the one mentioned in Jn 1.3: "all things were made by him," who has "mixed and compounded all things in all."

In the same way, whoever would interpret the term "all things" (*ta panta*) as if it referred to perceptible and material things, would be "deceiving." The term must refer instead to "all things" in their essential being, apart from the materiality that comes to be associated with them through the agency of the demiurge.

The Naassene exegete next considers Jn 1.4: "In him was life, and the life was the light of men." Here again, none of the terms are to be taken in their literal, or "simple," meaning. The term "life" cannot refer to the "life" of immediate physical existence, nor the "light" to the light of sense-experience, nor the "men" (*anthrōpoi*) to actual human beings. Those to whom the verse refers are primal and spiritual beings as they are in the primal Anthropos; the "life" that "comes to be" in him is the "ineffable race of perfect human beings (*anthrōpōn*)" (Ref 5.8.5).

The Naassene exegete explains that Jn 1.3*b* means that "what comes to be apart from him," is *nothing* (*to ouden*). This technical term for non-being he refers to the *cosmos idikos*, the sphere of materiality (Ref 5.8.5-6). This materiality, this "nothing," comes into being "apart from him" through the agency of the "fourth God," the creator of matter. The material sphere, excluded from the "all things" that

---

[1] For discussion, see A. Hilgenfeld, *Die Ketzergeschichte des Urchristentums* (Leipzig, 1884), 253; W. Bousset, *Hauptprobleme der Gnosis* (Göttingen, 1907), 240.

ontologically are, is *non-being,* and is said to be ruled by the demiurge Ialdabaoth.

In this way Jn 1.3, interwoven with citations from Jewish sources, from Homer, Herodotus, Plutarch, Paul, and other writings, becomes a "proof text" for the Naassene doctrine of the threefold nature of being. To discern this doctrine in such diverse sources, the exegete must first grasp the metaphysical principles outlined above. His exegetical task is to discern in each text to what principle of being or non-being each phrase refers.

Peratae exegesis

A similar exegesis of Jn 1.3 occurs in the works of a second group which Hippolytus classifies also among "ophite" gnostics. These, the Peratae, he says, claim to have been instructed "in the knowledge of necessity and causes of becoming," and to have come through these and "transcended" (*perasai*) them (Ref. 5.15.1–16.1). The Peratae claim to teach "a doctrine of Christ," and specifically to have constructed their theology from "the holy scriptures" (Ref 5.6.1). Apparently their group was not generally regarded as heretical among Christian circles. Hippolytus himself admits that "their blasphemy against Christ has for many years . . . gone unnoticed" (Ref 5.12.1). According to his account, they support their theology primarily from Genesis and John, referring occasionally to Exodus and Isaiah (they also cite a passage from the "Lord's prayer," without mentioning Matthew). The Peratae also acknowledge the spiritual insights of the Greek poets and philosophers such as Homer and Heraclitus. They teach that all things derive from a triad or trinity of three principles in one. The first of these they call the "perfect good," or "the unbegotten cosmos"; the second, "infinite self-generated potentiality," or the "self-generated cosmos"; the third, "eidetic or formal principle," or the "generated cosmos." On the basis of this structure, they distinguish three orders each of *theos,* of *logos,* of *nous,* and of *anthrōpos,* respectively.[2]

---

[2] Ref 5.12.2-3: οὗτοι φάσκουσι τὸν κόσμον εἶναι ἕνα, τριχῇ διῃρημένον. ἔστι δὲ τῆς τριχῇ διαιρέσεως παρ' αὐτοῖς τὸ μὲν ἕν μέρος οἷον μία τις ἀρχή, καθάπερ πηγὴ μεγάλη εἰς ἀπείρους τῷ λόγῳ τμηθῆναι τομὰς δυναμένη· ἡ δὲ πρώτη τομὴ καὶ προσεχεστέρα κατ' αὐτούς ἐστι τριὰς καὶ καλεῖται ἀγαθὸν τέλειον, μέγεθος πατρικόν. τὸ δὲ δεύτερον τῆς τριάδος αὐτῶν μέρος οἱονεὶ δυνάμεων ἄπειρόν τι πλῆθος ἐξ αὐτῶν γεγενημένων· τὸ τρίτον ἰδικόν. καὶ ἔστι τὸ μὲν πρῶτον ἀγέννητον ὅπερ ἐστὶν ἀγαθόν· τὸ δὲ δεύτερον ἀγαθὸν αὐτογενές· τὸ τρίτον γεννητόν· ὅθεν διαρρήδην λέγουσι τρεῖς θεούς, τρεῖς λόγους, τρεῖς νοῦς, τρεῖς ἀνθρώπους.

Their exegetical explanation of the apparent verbal contradiction between Jn 3.17 and 2 Cor 11.3, for example, shows how their meta-physical principle functions hermeneutically. The first passage says that the son of man has come into the "cosmos" not to destroy the "cosmos" but to save it. The first occurrence of the term, they explain, refers to the "self-generated cosmos"; the second to the "unengendered cosmos." The passage in 2 Corinthians, on the other hand, expressing the hope "that we may not be destroyed along with the cosmos," refers to the third, "eidetic cosmos," which, being material, is bound for destruction (Ref 5.12.5-7).

When the Peratae consider Jn 1.3, they, like the Naassenes, reject any immediate interpretation of the terms. They introduce this passage into a discussion of the "great arche," the arche of "all things." The meaning of "all things" is explained by taking Jn 1.4 as parenthetical to 1.3. The term "life" of 1.4 they take as a reference to Eve, "mother of all living beings"; thus "all things" share a common nature (Ref 5.16.12-14). The agent "through whom" all come into existence is the son, whose creative activity is described. He is the mediating principle between the infinite, eternal being of the Father and the corruptible, specific existence of matter (Ref 5.17.1-10). Through the son all receive life. What comes into being "apart from him" (as in Naassene exegesis) is the material realm of non-being. Applying this principle to Jn 8.44, the exegete explains that the material realm is ruled by "the creator and ruler of matter"—the Johannine "ruler of this world."

Valentinian exegesis

Naassene and Peratae exegesis offers a basis for analogy and comparison with the far more sophisticated exegesis of the Valentinian gnostics. The Valentinians join the Naassenes and Peratae in rejecting the apologists' historical and typological theory of revelation. They do claim to accept both Jewish and Christian traditions, insofar as these are interpreted in accordance with their own theological and exegetical principles.[3] The Valentinians also develop exegetical techniques that enable them to surpass the mere literal reading of "scripture" as a nar-

---

[3] N. Brox, *Offenbarung, Gnosis, und gnostischer Mythos bei Irenäus von Lyon* (Salzburg, 1966), 22 f, points out that the Valentinians, according to Irenaeus' testimony, claim to be members of the same church, believers in the common doctrine (see above, pp. 11 f) who have been unjustly excluded from the community on account of their esoteric interpretations of that doctrine.

ration of actual events, and to disclose the "deeper mysteries" hidden under the literal meaning of the texts.[4]

As noted above, Irenaeus relates that the "heretics," above all the Valentinians, seized especially on the Johannine gospel, considering it compatible in style and conception with their own theology (AH 3.10.1–11.2) and making extensive use of it to illustrate their metaphysical doctrines (AH 3.11.7). Whether Valentinus himself knew and used the gospel is uncertain[5]; but the extant exegetical fragments from Ptolemy, Heracleon, and Theodotus amply confirm Irenaeus' statement.

Yet investigation of such fragments has confronted scholars with a difficult problem. How can we account for the fact that these sources— apparently all "Valentinian"—offer such different exegeses of the same Johannine passages? An example of this problem occurs in the case of three variant Valentinian interpretations of Jn 1.3: (1) Ptolemy, in his commentary on the Johannine prologue, interprets this verse in terms of the myth of the pleromic aions (AH 1.8.5). (2) Theodotus refers the same verse to the savior, who, having emerged from the pleroma, constitutes Sophia in the *kenoma,* the "emptiness" or void (Exc 45.3). (3) Heracleon refers the same verse to the creation of the cosmos (CJ 2.14). The problem is not simply that these three different commentators offer different interpretations of the same passage. It becomes more complex when we recognize that the same commentator sometimes offers variant exegeses of the same verse in his different writings. Ptolemy's Letter to Flora, for example, gives an exegesis of Jn 1.3 parallel to Heracleon's—and entirely different from Ptolemy's own exegesis of the verse in his prologue commentary!

Three views on this problem emerge from scholarly analysis. The first notes these differences without attempting to reconcile them in relation to one another, as "evidence that the (Valentinian) exegete does not consider himself bound to a single definitive interpretation." [6] De Faye sets forth a second view, attempting to understand the different Valentinian exegeses of Jn 1.3 in terms of an internal theological development within the Valentinian school. He claims that Ptolemy and Heracleon exemplify an increasingly complex christology set within a "strictly monotheistic" system. De Faye suggests that their develop-

---

[4]Cf C. Barth, *Die Interpretation des Neuen Testaments in der valentinianischen Gnosis* (Texte und Untersuchungen 37.3 [1911]), 52: "The endeavor of the Valentinian exegete must be to recognize where such secrets lie hidden, and to disclose the mystical meaning of the discourse."

[5] Loewenich, *Johannes-Verständnis,* 72-74; Sanders, *Fourth Gospel,* 33 f.

[6] Barth, *Interpretation,* 98.

ment of Valentinian theology affords a greater role for the demiurge and a more positive evaluation of the cosmos than did earlier Valentinian tradition. The exegesis of Jn 1.3 which occurs in the prologue commentary, then, would represent an early formulation adhering more closely to the theology of Valentinus himself. Heracleon's commentary on John, by contrast, would represent a more theologically developed Valentinianism.[7]

Those scholars who, following de Faye, hail Heracleon's "move toward orthodoxy" have in mind the contrast between Heracleon's exegesis of Jn 1.3 and that of Ptolemy's prologue commentary.[8] They are assuming, moreover, that these two interpretations of the same verse must be mutually exclusive. This assumption encounters serious difficulties when the texts are re-examined. In the first place, this argument violates the internal consistency of Heracleon's exegesis of John. Heracleon not only does refer to the *pleroma* and the *kenoma,* but also places definite limits to the scope of the exegesis he offers of Jn 1.3. Secondly, this "developmental theory" cannot account for the fact that in his Letter to Flora Ptolemy himself gives an interpretation of Jn 1.3 wholly different from that of his own commentary—and entirely congruent with Heracleon's interpretation.

Von Loewenich, acknowledging this, suggests a third approach: either to dispute Ptolemy's authorship of the prologue commentary without attempting to reconcile the exegeses of the presumed "different authors," or (since the evidence for Ptolemy's authorship seems sound) to attribute the discrepancies to the "arbitrary nature of gnostic exegesis."[9]

In order to evaluate these views, we may begin by analyzing the different exegeses of Jn 1.3 in terms of the fundamental principles of Valentinian theology. Such an analysis indicates that these different in-

---

[7] *Gnostiques,* 108 and 79.

[8] Cf Brooke, *Fragments,* 50 n. 1: "The teaching of Heracleon is more nearly allied to that of Irenaeus . . . as against the ordinary Valentinian interpretation of this passage." Von Loewenich, *Johannes-Verständnis,* 84: "Heracleon is compelled, through his exegetical knowledge, to free himself from the other dogmatic gnostic interpretation as it confronts us in AH 1.8.5." So also Sanders, *Fourth Gospel,* 64, noting that "Irenaeus stresses the full impact of the 'all things' against the Valentinians, who were inclined to limit its scope," concludes that "Heracleon is an exception. He says that the Logos is . . . the one by whom the world came into being. . . . Heracleon's Valentinianism was profoundly modified by his understanding of the Fourth Gospel."

[9] *Johannes-Verständnis,* 76: "The interpretation of Jn 1.3 is here (AH 1.8.5) entirely different from that in the Letter to Flora. When one considers, however, the arbitrariness of the gnostic in exegesis, one may not on this basis alone dispute the author's identity."

terpretations of the same verse, far from indicating either an "arbitrary" or a "developed" exegetical practice, actually conform to a consistent theological structure. The Valentinian threefold theological principle leads to the development of a threefold exegetical schema, according to which the same verse may be interpreted in each of three correlated frames of reference.[10] These correspond to the three stages of the Valentinian myth of redemption: first, the *pleroma;* second, the *kenoma;* and third, the *cosmos.* The extant fragments offer examples of exegesis of Jn 1.3 in terms of each of these frames of reference. Ptolemy's exegesis of the prologue (paralleled in the Excerpts from Theodotus, 6.1-4) interprets the verse in terms of the *pleroma.* Exc 45.1-3 interprets it in terms of the *kenoma.* Heracleon (and Ptolemy in his Letter) interprets it as well in terms of the *cosmos.*

To begin with Ptolemy's prologue commentary, we note that he introduces the prologue as the work of "John, the Lord's disciple." [11] John, he says, intends to "tell the genesis of the whole *(tōn holōn)*." This term, used technically, here designates the pleroma,[12] as Ptolemy specifies in line 6 (AH 1.8.5). John, he says, posits a primal principle *(archē)* which is also called "son," "monogenes," and "theos." This *Arche,* being generated from "the Father," bears within himself seminally *(spermatikōs)* the whole of the pleroma. Then the Logos is generated in turn from the Arche, bearing within himself "the whole being of the aions," which he himself (the Logos) later "formed." [13]

Now we can see how Ptolemy's introduction has gone far beyond a statement that the author intends to describe the genesis of the pleroma. He actually has summarized the theory of the threefold creation that his exegesis is to expound, and has outlined the triadic monism of the Godhead in hierarchical form. With skill and brevity, he (no

[10] Sagnard (*Gnose,* 481-520) and G. Quispel (*Lettre à Flora,* Sources Chrétiennes 24 [1966], 72-73) have indicated this structure.

[11] Sanders (*Fourth Gospel,* 37) points out that the Valentinians may have been the first to ascribe the fourth gospel to "John."

[12] K. Müller, *Beiträge zum Verständnis der valentinischen Gnosis* 1/5 (in: Nachrichten von der Königl. Gesell. der Wiss. zu Göttingen, phil.-hist. Klasse 1920) , 180 f.

[13] AH 1.8.5: "Ετι δὲ 'Ιωάννην τὸν μαθητὴν τοῦ κυρίου διδάσκουσι τὴν πρώτην 'Ογδοάδα μεμηνυκέναι, αὐταῖς λέξεσι λέγοντες οὕτως· 'Ιωάννης, ὁ μαθητὴς τοῦ κυρίου, βουλόμενος εἰπεῖν τὴν τῶν ὅλων γένεσιν, καθ' ἣν τὰ πάντα προέβαλεν ὁ Πατήρ, ἀρχήν τινα ὑποτίθεται τὸ πρῶτον γεννηθὲν ὑπὸ τοῦ θεοῦ, ὃ δὴ καὶ Υἱὸν καὶ Μονογενῆ καὶ θεὸν κέκληκεν, ἐν ᾧ τὰ πάντα ὁ Πατὴρ προέβαλε σπερματικῶς. ὑπὸ δὲ τούτου φησὶ τὸν Λόγον προβεβλῆσθαι καὶ ἐν αὐτῷ τὴν ὅλην τῶν Αἰώνων οὐσίαν, ἣν αὐτὸς ὕστερον ἐμόρφωσεν ὁ Λόγος. ἐπεὶ οὖν περὶ πρώτης γενέσεως λέγει, καλῶς ἀπὸ τῆς ἀρχῆς, τουτέστιν τοῦ Υἱοῦ καὶ τοῦ Λόγου, τὴν διδασκαλίαν ποιεῖται.

less than the Ophites) has "initiated" the reader into the structural principles of Valentinian gnosis. Then, reiterating the distinction already drawn between *arche* and *logos,* Ptolemy continues: ". . . since, then, he is speaking of the first genesis, he does well to begin his teaching from the Arche, that is, the son; and from the Logos." Next he cites Jn 1.1-2, pointing out how John

> . . . first distinguishes between the three, *theos, arche,* and *logos,* and again unites them so that he may show the projection of each of the two, that of the son and that of the *logos,* and simultaneously their union with each other and with the father. For the *arche* is both *in* the father and *of* the father, and the *logos,* in turn, both *in* the *arche* and *of* the *arche.*

The following verse (Jn 1.2) shows, he says, that "the Logos" is related to the Father "through the Arche." For being generated from the *arche-theos,* the Logos can be called *theos* as well, on the principle he states. The summary statement, Jn 1.2, shows the order of the hierarchy:

(1) The Father, who "emits all things";
(2) The Arche, also called *monogenes* and *theos,* being "generated from *theos";*
(3) The Logos, also called *theos,* for the same reason.[14]

Ptolemy then exegetes Jn 1.3 by saying that "therefore the logos became the cause of the formation and genesis to all the other aions." His premise is the metaphysical theory that *being* and *knowing* are exact correlates. What exists "seminally" in the mind (the *arche,* or *monogenes,* is also called *nous*) must be given "form" in order to be rendered rationally comprehensible, or, synonymously, actually existent.[15] As Irenaeus relates this doctrine, "the cause of the external duration for the rest of the aions is the incomprehensible transcendence of the Father, from whom their being *(ousia)* derives"; and, on the other hand, "the cause of their origination and formation is his comprehensibility, which is the Son" (AH 1.1.4). The Logos therefore, from the *ousia* he receives, directly causes their existence and formation, whereby he is called "father of all the aions who come into existence after him, and arche of the whole pleroma" (AH 1.1.1).

This exegesis of the Johannine prologue is identical with the abridged version transcribed in the Excerpts from Theodotus 6-7*a,* an observation which supports the view that Valentinian exegesis, far

---

[14] Cf AH 1.8.5: Apparently paraphrasing Jn 3.6, Ptolemy says, "for what is born of God, is God (τὸ γὰρ ἐκ θεοῦ γεννηθὲν θεός ἐστιν) ."

[15] Sagnard, *Gnose,* 313-315.

from being "arbitrary" or "idiosyncratic" (as the heresiologists often charge) follows a consistent and traditional pattern.

In Exc 45.3, however, the verse occurs not in the context of the *pleroma* but of the *kenoma*. Here it receives a wholly different interpretation. A description of the savior, sent out from the pleroma into the kenoma, forms the context. He goes to deliver the lower Sophia from her alienation. First separating her from her "passions" (*pathē*) he heals and liberates her from them, and confers on her the "formation of gnosis," teaching her of the beings in the pleroma up to herself (Exc 45.1). As she grasps this understanding, she "comes into existence." Then the savior takes the passions which he has separated from her (which are in an incorporeal and random state) and transforms them into an incorporeal matter, then into a compound substance, and finally into bodies. By this process he brings into being the elements of the "second ordinance."

So through the appearance of the savior the Sophia comes into being, and the external elements are created. Thereby the savior becomes the first universal creator, and the Sophia the second (Exc 47.1).

Within this second exegetical context, the "all things" of Jn 1.3 refers not to the pleromic aions, but to the "external elements." The phrase "through him" refers not to the pleromic Logos but to the savior. The verb "came into being" refers not to the formation of divine being (*ousia*) into pleromic hypostases, but to the formation of the "passions" into matter and finally into bodies. Here the savior, Sophia, and the demiurge of Exc 46, whom Sophia creates, are all designated as "creators" on different levels. That this passage and Irenaeus' parallel account derive, in all probability, from a common source document, makes it especially necessary to resolve the apparent contradiction between this exegesis and that of the prologue commentary.

Finally, Ptolemy's Letter to Flora offers a third exegesis of Jn 1.3. This time neither the pleroma nor the kenoma but the *cosmos* forms the context. Here the verse receives a third exegesis—one that seems, at first glance, incongruous with Valentinian theology. For when Ptolemy had interpreted the "all things" of Jn 1.3 as the pleroma, Irenaeus had attacked his exegesis, insisting that the term must refer not to the pleroma, but to "this world and to everything in it." [16] "All

---

[16] AH 3.11.7: "'All things,' he says, 'were made by him'; therefore in 'all things' this creation of ours is included; for we cannot concede to these men (the Valentinians) that the words 'all things' are said in reference to those within their pleroma."

things," Irenaeus insists, means "this creation." Irenaeus cites Jn 1.11 to prove that the world the savior enters into is called "his own" (AH 5.18.2). The objection, directed as it is against the exegesis of the prologue commentary, makes a valid point. In the treatise he addresses to Flora, however, Ptolemy offers an interpretation identical to the one Irenaeus gives. He refers the "all things" to the cosmos and (like Irenaeus) supports this exegesis by reference to Jn 1.11 (Ep 3.26).

Ptolemy's opening discussion of the different views of God, and consequently of the world and the law, forms the context. There are some, he says, who attribute the law—and presumably also the creation of the world, as these are parallel throughout the passage—to "God the Father" himself. Others, diametrically opposed, ascribe the law to the devil, as they also attribute to him the creation of the world, saying that he is the "father and maker of the cosmos" (Ep. 3.6). Both views miss the truth. The law, imperfect and incomplete as it is (according to the savior's own words), cannot have been given by "the perfect Father," any more than, being just, it can be attributed to the "unjust adversary." At this point, having set up the problem, Ptolemy introduces the "apostle" John as an authority who has "destroyed in advance the inconsistent 'wisdom' of these liars." Ptolemy has already linked *cosmos* and *nomos* in his argument, so that when he introduces Jn 1.3 as scriptural evidence to support his reasoning about the cosmos, he infers from this a similar conclusion about the law: ". . . since the creation . . . is his own, all things have come into being through him, and without him nothing came into being." Context and introductory statement indicate that the phrase "his own" here refers to the creation of the cosmos. But Ptolemy later calls the "just and evil-hating God" the "creator and maker of all the world and its contents" (Ep 9.4).

The problem with this interpretation is that while the first line of the passage in 3.6 ascribes the creation to the savior, the passage goes on to call the "just God" creator of the world.[17] Exc 46-50, which describes three interrelated creators participating in the world's creation, suggests a resolution of this difficulty. If Ptolemy shares this conception of three creators—the Sophia, who produces the basic materials; the

---

[17] On the generally accepted reading of ἰδίαν with the αὐτοῦ (Cod. Vat. graec. 503/Cod. Marc. graec. 125), the phrase refers to the savior of 3.5; i.e., the savior comes into "his own" world (cf Jn 1.11). Harnack (*Ptolemaeus' Brief an die Flora*, Bonn 1904), however, reads θείαν instead of ἰδίαν, taking the phrase as referring to the demiurge, and the third phrase as adjectival. Apparently he makes this suggestion not primarily on textual grounds, but to solve the problem of the "two creators" by making the passage refer only to one. His emendation is unnecessary if the hypothesis suggested below is accepted.

savior, who "forms" both Sophia and the "materials" of her passion; and Jahweh, who "orders" the materials and governs the world—this passage of the Letter becomes comprehensible. The creation is then the savior's "own creation," although the demiurge creates in an immediate sense.[18] This view is paralleled not only in the Excerpts, but also in Heracleon's interpretation of the creation. Reading the passage with this insight, we can see how Ptolemy interprets Jn 1.3 according to the triadic principle of his theology, and thereby claims to find in it evidence for the three orders of being he summarizes in AH 1.8.5: the transcendent Father, the savior of 3.6, and the demiurge.

If the exegesis of Jn 1.3 is shown to be internally self-consistent, there remains the problem of how the interpretation given here is related to that of the prologue commentary. The similarity of Ptolemy's exegesis of Jn 1.3 in his Letter to that of Heracleon's commentary on John has often been noted. This correlation is rather surprising. Apart from it, we might have constructed a hypothesis to account for the difference between Ptolemy's two exegeses on the basis of their formal context. According to such a hypothesis, Ptolemy might have intended to offer a simpler, more conventional exegesis in his introductory treatise to Flora, reserving his metaphysical doctrine for the instructed gnostic to read in the commentary. In that case we would expect to find a parallel between the two commentaries—Ptolemy's and Heracleon's —while both might differ from the popular and apologetic Letter. In fact, as noted above, we find the opposite. No immediate parallel appears between the two commentaries, while the parallel between the popular Letter and Heracleon's scholarly commentary is obvious.

Heracleon explains the "all things" of Jn 1.3 as "the cosmos and its contents." Conversely, he says, the statement that "apart from him nothing came into being" means "nothing of what is in the cosmos and creation" (CJ 2.14). Yet Heracleon takes care to specify that when he speaks of logos he refers not to the pleromic aion Logos, but to the savior who descends from the pleroma, and becomes the actual agent of creation. For he

. . . furnishes the cause of the genesis of the cosmos to the demiurge: therefore the cosmos comes into being "through him," that is, through the logos. This phrase, "through him" is not to be considered as though the logos, acting as agent, is energized by another; but that he himself is the operating agent of what another (the demiurge) makes.

[18] As Quispel says (Lettre, 73): "The author has in mind the Valentinian myth of the creation of the world, which recognizes three beings participating in the process of creation: Sophia, . . . the savior, . . . and Yahweh. So the creation of the world is the work of Christ and of Yahweh."

Now the parallel to the account in the Letter is complete. There Ptolemy had identified the savior as the agent described in Jn 1.3 as logos, "by whom" all things exist; and there also the discussion focuses exclusively on the creation of the cosmos. Both authors assume a common frame of reference. Heracleon, far from claiming the originality with which he has sometimes been credited, refers to his tradition as the authority for his exegesis.

These three different Valentinian interpretations of the verse—that of the prologue commentary, of Exc 45 f, and of Heracleon—can be seen to deal with three distinct stages or levels of mythic history, each dynamically devolving from the prior stage, and issuing finally in the creation of the cosmos.[19]

Seen in this perspective, Ptolemy's prologue commentary (as he himself carefully defines its scope) moves wholly within the *pleromic* sphere. Each word of the verse finds its pleromic referent, showing how "all things," that is, the aions, come into being through the logos of the primary tetrad. The description in Exc 45 f (of the savior descending to the lower Sophia) refers, then, to the second stage of the process: here the "all things" consist of Sophia and the elements, while the agent is the savior, also called *christos* and *logos*. Devolving from this extra-pleromic act of creation is the framework of cosmic creation, for which the structural elements (i.e., the higher operating agent, the demiurge, and the materials) have been furnished. Finally, Ptolemy's Letter and Heracleon's commentary show how Jn 1.3 applies to this third, cosmic creation, where "all things" means "the cosmos and its contents," which come into being through the logos energizing the demiurge.

The difference between Ptolemy's exegesis in the Letter and in his prologue commentary represent, then, not primarily the different levels of gnosis (although this is also implied) but primarily different definitions of the intended framework of the exegesis. Heracleon's exegesis, similarly, evinces a decision to confine his interpretation to the framework of the *cosmic* creation. Recognizing that his exegesis consistently operates within this framework, however, are we correct in assuming that he shares the common Valentinian tradition which includes the two "higher levels" of mythic history? The details of his commentary show that he does, and show moreover how the principle of an ontological trinity (corresponding to the three levels of the Valentinian myth) functions as his basic hermeneutical principle. Apparently each stage of the mythic history can supply a total framework for the inter-

---

[19] For summary, see Sagnard, *Gnose*, 481-520.

31

pretation of this verse. The task of the exegete is to discern precisely to which agent and to which object each phrase refers in the context within which he is working. Some passages, however, seem to be regarded as specifically appropriate to certain contexts. For example, when Ptolemy interprets the prologue in terms of the *pleroma,* he omits the verses that mention John the baptist, resuming the text again at Jn 1.14. The passage omitted here (which *is* discussed when the prologue is interpreted in kenomic or cosmic terms) he may not have considered relevant to the pleromic level. Heracleon, on the other hand, who focuses on the *cosmic* context, follows the text systematically without omitting verses. It is as though—spurred by anti-Valentinian criticism—he has resolved to offer a Valentinian exegesis of the whole gospel in terms of the cosmic context alone. Yet he offers no basis for speculating on whether his motives are apologetic. Exegesis of the gospel in terms of the cosmic level apparently formed an integral element of the total process of Valentinian exegesis. Heracleon's decision to write a commentary on a single text, taking up each verse in sequence, may explain his decision to work within the cosmic context; i.e., some passages (such as those on John the baptist) may not bear a pleromic interpretation, while every verse may have a cosmic interpretation. Further consideration of Heracleon's intention, however, is to be deferred to the conclusion of the analysis of his exegesis.

To test the hypothesis that the different Valentinian exegeses of the same verse actually offer interrelated, complementary exegeses based on a common theological structure, we shall next examine the different Valentinian exegeses of Jn 1.4 in the extant sources, turning first to Ptolemy's prologue exegesis. Ptolemy, having described the pleromic Logos as creator of all the other aions, then considers the relation of Jn 1.4 to this process. This verse, in his view, indicates the process of creation in the pleroma. It indicates how the pleromic aion Zoe comes into being in Logos, her syzygos (AH 1.8.5). Logos and Zoe together constitute one being, as complementary aspects of a single process, described in the metaphor of conception and birth.[20] As Logos, the

---

[20] For this reason, the couple can be understood where only the male member is specifically named, as the couple Ecclesia-Anthropos is understood from the mention of Anthropos alone in Jn 1.4*b*, and there in the plural. Ptolemy recognizes that the explicit level of the text recounts the savior's descent into the extrapleromic *topos;* yet his own understanding of gnosis enables him to read here the deeper level of meaning, which he says refers to the genesis of the first ogdoad. The Valentinians could appreciate the very intricacy of this argument not as evidence of its "contrived" character (as Irenaeus and Origen charge) but of Ptolemy's exegetical skill; see Sagnard, *Gnose,* 312 f.

male element, is said to "give form to" the aions (as the male sperm, according to contemporary biological theory, was thought to "give form to" the fetus), so the female element Zoe "fructifies" and "gives life to" their offspring. Logos and Zoe together, then, are called the "parents" and "makers of the pleroma," bringing forth the next syzygic pair of aions, Anthropos and Ecclesia (AH 2.13.8).

How Jn 1.4 could receive a second complementary exegesis in terms of the dynamics of the kenoma is indicated in AH 1.4.1 and its parallel, Exc 6.3. Here, in the context of the savior's descent from the pleroma into the kenoma, the Valentinian exegete takes Jn 1.4 to refer to the process of Sophia's redemption. The savior descending to her, becomes her "light and life" (*phōs kai zōē*, AH 1.4.1). Uniting with her, he brings to birth in her the "life" (*zōē*) which is also called the "seed," the "images of the pleromic aions," which are destined ultimately to be restored to the pleroma (AH 2.20.3). The exegesis of Jn 1.4 within this second context explains, then, how Christ in the kenoma, bearing Logos and Zoe within himself, unites with Sophia to bring forth the "image" of the pleromic syzygy Anthropos-Ecclesia. This syzygy, being the antitype of the pleromic aion, nevertheless is still, at this level, the archetype of the future Anthropos-Ecclesia that is to come into being at the third stage of creation, in the cosmos.

The emergence of Anthropos-Ecclesia in the kenoma as the "pneumatic seed" prefigures the future emergence of its cosmic counterpart. The "seed," being "of the same nature" as the savior, is to be "implanted" in those persons who, in the future cosmic creation, will constitute the *anthropos-ecclesia* in the cosmos. Sown secretly into the human soul "by an ineffable providence," they will grow up and reach perfection as the cosmic antitype of the kenomic syzygy (AH 1.5.1). For this reason, as Theodotus says, "The ecclesia is said to have been chosen before the foundation of the cosmos" (Exc 41.1). This becomes the mythic background for the Valentinian doctrine of the ecclesia as the "elect."

What is structurally the same process recurs at each stage of devolution. It recurs finally at the third stage in the process of creation—the creation of the cosmos. Within this third context, Jn 1.4 received a third exegesis. This time it is taken as referring to the emergence of divine "life" in the cosmos. The Excerpts and the Fragments of Heracleon offer substantially the same interpretation—an interpretation simultaneously christological and soteriological. According to Exc 6.4, the "life" (*zōē*) that comes into being in the cosmos is the savior. Jn 11.25 and 14.6 are cited to show that he himself calls himself "the life" (Exc 6.3). He "comes into being" within "every anthropos" (cf Jn 1.9), that is, within every member of the "pneumatic seed" that originates from the archetypal Anthropos-Ecclesia.

Heracleon likewise explains that "the life" of Jn 1.4 refers to the savior, who is the divine life. The phrase "in him," taken in the cosmic context, means "within the pneumatic men (*anthrōpous*)." Like the exegete of the Excerpts, Heracleon assumes that the savior and those human beings who are "pneumatics" are essentially identical. To explain this, he refers to their pre-cosmic origin. They have, he says, been "sown" as "seed" by the logos, receiving thereby their "first form of genesis." When the logos enters into the cosmos as savior, he brings the "seed" into its second "formation," which is "enlightenment," and restores it to its "own identity" (*perigraphēn idian*; CJ 2.21).

The theological basis of Valentinian hermeneutics

From this outline we can see how Jn 1.4 as well as 1.3 receives three distinct and complementary interpretations. The basic methodological principle of Valentinian exegesis is that the exegete must define precisely in terms of which context—pleromic, kenomic, or cosmic—he intends to interpret any given verse. So when Ptolemy sets forth the pleromic interpretation of the prologue, he selects for exegesis only those verses from which he can trace the members of the first ogdoad. In this context, the references he makes to the christological and soteriological interpretation of these verses remain only peripheral to his primary exegetical aim. Such exegetical decisions are grounded theologically on the ontological trinitarianism which is expressed mythically in terms of the pleroma, the kenoma, and the cosmos. Knowledge of the myth and its theological basis forms the essential prerequisite for understanding Valentinian exegesis.

The exegetical methodology of their opponents, conversely, also emerges from a specific theological perspective. So Justin claims that the gospels are and must be understood to be "memoirs"—witnesses to actual events—and not poetic fictions or mythologically expressed allegory. He and Hippolytus insist that, in witnessing to unique events, these writings—including both the Jewish prophecies which anticipate them, and the gospels which attest them—must be, as a source of revelation, unique. They are not to be compared with any other writings, whether poetic or philosophic. Since it is in the actual *events* that revelation occurs, what the gospels testify can be superceded neither by any inner intuitive or mystical experience, nor by independently derived metaphysical principles.

Such apologists for the mainstream position as Irenaeus, Hippolytus, Clement, and Origen clearly have little interest in examining gnostic exegesis on its own terms. They denounce it as "arbitrary," and "contrived," or "irrational"—accusations certainly appropriate for their polemical intention. Their assessment, however, has too often been adopted and repeated by students of early Christian history. When Valentinian exegesis is investigated in terms of its own theological principles, however, the diverse fragments of exegesis, even the apparently contradictory interpretations of the same verse, can be seen to derive from a consistent theological structure.

Three Valentinian exegeses of Jn 1.3-4 correlated

Pleroma	*Kenoma*	*Cosmos*
Jn 1.3—cf AH 1.8.5; Exc 6.1-4	—cf Exc 45.3 f	—cf Letter to Flora; CJ 2.14
panta=the primal aion, the pleroma	panta=the elements (τὰ ἔξω), Sophia	panta=the cosmos (and its contents)
di' autou=the Logos of the Tetrad	di' autou=the Savior sent as "fruit of the pleroma" into the kenoma	di' autou=the logos that is revealed in cosmic creation, and savior in the cosmos
egeneto=came into being (οὐσία) and form (μορφή)	egeneto=came into being and form	egeneto=came into being and form
Jn 1.4—cf AH 1.8.5	—cf AH 1.4.1; Exc 6.3	—cf Exc 6.4; CJ 2.21
en autō=in the Logos of the Tetrad	en autō=in the savior, "fruit of the pleroma"	en autō=in the savior in the cosmos and in "pneumatic anthrōpoi"
egeneto=came into being and form	egeneto=came into being and form	egeneto=came into being and form
zōē=Zoe, syzygos of the Logos in the Tetrad	zōē=the restored Sophia, syzygos of the savior, archetype of the ecclesia	zōē=the savior who is the pneumatic "life" of the pneumatics (ecclesia)

2. The Johannine Prologue in Valentinian Exegesis

With this introduction to their presuppositions and methodology, one may now turn to examine Valentinian exegesis of the Johannine prologue as a whole.

This requires us to examine the passages of Valentinian prologue exegesis that Clement, Irenaeus, and Origen record. But the polemical context in which these passages occur cannot be ignored. Although the heresiologists use different methods and arguments to attack Valentinian exegesis, examination of their arguments can clarify the ways in which these theologians polemically misinterpret Valentinian exegesis. It also can guide us to the central issues at stake in the controversy. First we must consider what Clement and Irenaeus say about Valentinian prologue exegesis, and on what basis they criticize it. Following this, we may investigate Heracleon's prologue exegesis. Finally, analysis of Origen's attack on Heracleon may indicate what issues have become —by Origen's time—central to the hermeneutical controversy over John.

We have already seen how Ptolemy interprets Jn 1.1-4, and how he (having decided on the pleromic framework for his exegesis) has selected for comment only those passages which he considers refer to the pleroma. His theological instruction into the "mystery" of the tetrads enables Ptolemy to recognize that Jn 1.4 signifies the second tetrad. It indicates, he explains, the emergence of Zoe in her syzygos Anthropos (AH 1.8.5). This indicates in *pleromic* terms how the elect emerge in the unfolding of the divine life. Another such passage that bears reference to the pleroma is Jn 1.14. In this passage (which appears to be a rather rhetorical praise of the savior) Ptolemy finds hidden reference to the primary pleromic tetrad, consisting of the Father, Charis, Monogenes, and Aletheia. He perceives (according to his initiation into Valentinian theology) that in Jn 1.14 John "clearly sets forth the first tetrad, when he speaks of the Father and Charis, and Monogenes and Aletheia." Secondly, Ptolemy notes that the verse may *also* refer to the savior as he appears in the kenoma, as "fruit of the pleroma," bearing within himself the powers of all the aions, so that he "can be called by the names of all of them" (including Monogenes, Aletheia, and Charis). Thirdly, the verse may be taken to refer to the "logos made flesh, whose glory we beheld," that is, to the savior manifested in material form in the cosmos. As no corporeality exists either in the pleroma or in the kenoma, the savior comes into visible form only as he enters into the cosmos and assumes the existence of the psychic Christ and the body of Jesus. Ptolemy calls this visible form of the savior "logos made flesh," adding, "his glory we beheld, and his glory was such as that of the Monogenes, being given to him of the Father." He intends this comment, apparently, as an explanatory paraphrase of Jn 1.14. That the glory of the "logos made flesh" is similar to that of the Monogenes (but distinct from and lesser than it) recalls the divine hierarchy that Ptolemy previously has established. Not only is the visible logos himself *not* the Monogenes, but he is separated from him by whole realms of being.[1]

The contrast between the "logos made flesh" and the pleromic Monogenes of Jn 1.18 is drawn even more sharply in the parallel to this passage in Exc 7.3. Here the Valentinian exegete stresses the phrase "like the Monogenes," apparently with polemical intent against those who consider the mere cosmic manifestation of the logos to be identical

---

[1] To reiterate the scheme Ptolemy presents here: The Monogenes who issues from the Father and communes with him alone reveals to the other pleromic aions this gnosis. He also brings forth the Logos through whom the other aions come into being. From this pleroma (now seen as a single totality) the savior emerges into the darkness and constitutes there the ogdoadic *topos* ruled by Sophia. From her, in turn, comes the demiurge, and below the ogdoad the seven heavens of Jahweh, and finally the cosmos he creates. Into that cosmos the savior himself penetrates, taking the soul of the demiurge's son—and this person is the *logos made flesh* through whose diminished image the likeness of pleromic being still shines.

with the pleromic Monogenes of the primary tetrad. The writer states that the Monogenes of the tetrad remains eternally in the Father, having emanated from him, concluding that "the one seen here is no longer 'Monogenes' but 'like the Monogenes,' as the apostle declares" (cf Jn 1.14; Exc 7.3) .[2]

Clement's attack on Valentinian exegesis

Clement of Alexandria, as the Excerpts indicate, was acquainted with Valentinian exegesis of John from several sources.[3] Clement chooses not to dispute with the Valentinians over hermeneutics. Instead he attacks directly the metaphysical structure of their theology in order to reassert the oneness of God throughout his manifestations. From this he develops a theory of spiritual being (*ousia*). He intends thereby to reinterpret the Johannine prologue in terms of the theological claims of the "mainstream" Christian community. "We say that the same divine logos is in God, who is also said to be 'in the bosom of the Father' (Jn 1.18), continually, wholly, one God" (Exc 8.1). He begins with this sweeping assertion that the logos of 1.1 is identical with that of 1.18 which concludes the prologue. He indicates (without explaining it here) that the "logos in the archē" is thereby "in God." In this way he denies that the term *archē* indicates a mediate stage between the logos and the Father: instead he refers *archē* to the Father himself. Clement himself has coined the technical term "the identical logos-theos" (*ho en tautotēti logos theos*) to indicate the absolute identity of the logos throughout the differing predicates. This is the same logos, he continues, who creates "all things" (Jn 1.3), fulfilling, in Valentinian terms, the function of the pleromic Logos as well as that of the Arche-Monogenes. When he adds that by "all things" he understands "spiritual and intelligible and sensible reality" (Exc 6-7) he claims far more. Now the "identical logos" enacts all the activity which the Valentinians ascribe not only to the pleromic Logos, but also to the logos in the kenoma, to Sophia, and to the demiurge. Clement

---

[2] Cf Exc 7.3: The author contrasts the "Monogenes" who "remained in the bosom of the Father" (Jn 1.18) with "the one seen here," that is, Jesus, who is *not* the "Monogenes," but is "like" him.

[3] One of these sources was from Theodotus or his school, as both direct quotation formulae (cf Exc 1.1-2; 1.3; 1.16; 1.17; etc.) and parallelism of doctrine indicate. O. Dibelius has shown ("Studien zur Geschichte der Valentinianer," *Zeitschrift für die neutestamentliche Wissenschaft* **9** [1908], 230 f) that section 42-65 probably refers to the same source as does Irenaeus' account. See also C. Barth, *Interpretation*, 11 f.

intends his claim to annihilate the whole Valentinian schema of the three distinct "realms" or stages of being.

The theory of spiritual being which follows, however, offers certain difficulties. Exc 10-17 seems to set forth (in Casey's words) "a theory of radical materialism" quite alien to Clement's generally Platonic metaphysics.[4] This common view of the section ignores, however, Clement's own warning against a materialistic interpretation. It also ignores Clement's own intention in this section, which is to show how *all* beings (including the son himself) are constituted in distinction from the Father. The logos' very definition as *logos-theos* involves his distinction from "the God" (*ho theos*). This distinction consists in being constituted in terms of one's "own form and body" (Exc 10.1). Clement quickly adds that he does not mean "form" or "body" in a physical sense, but rather as one's own "idea" or "being" (Exc 10.3),[5] that is, constitution as a distinct entity. Having established this, he can show how the logos, although distinct from the Father "by definition" (*kata perigraphēn*) nevertheless shares with him identity of being (*ousia*).[6] This metaphysical discussion affords Clement a basis for claiming the unity of God in creation and revelation.

Clement realizes how difficult it is to speak of these distinctions in God while maintaining the absolute identity of the logos. Therefore, to convey his meaning, he uses the prologue verses in an unexpected and paradoxical way—a way exactly antithetical to the finely graded arrangement of Valentinian exegesis. He uses the very same verse that the Valentinians had referred to the *lowest* form of the logos' self-manifestation (Jn 1.14) to refer not only to the logos incarnate, but also to the logos as creator and prophetic revealer, and even to the *pre-existent* logos, who, according to Valentinian theology, stood at the

---

[4] R. P. Casey, *The Excerpta ex Theodoto of Clement of Alexandria* (London, 1934), 11. P. Collomp, "Une Source de Clement d'Alexandrie," *Revue de Phil. et Lit. et d'Histoire Anciennes* 37 (1913), 19 f, suggests a non-Valentinian and non-Clement source. W. Bousset (*Jüdisch-christlicher Schulbetrieb in Alexandria und Rom* [Göttingen, 1915], 161) suggests that the section may be from Pantaenus' lecture notes. Casey argues against Bousset's theory and for Clement's authorship on textual grounds (*Excerpta*, 8 f).

[5] Cf Exc 10.3: ἐκεῖ δὲ ὁ μὲν μονογενὴς καὶ ἰδίως νοερὸς ἰδέᾳ ἰδίᾳ καὶ οὐσίᾳ ἰδίᾳ κεχρημένος ἄκρως εἰλικρινεῖ καὶ ἡγεμονικωτάτῃ καὶ προσεχῶς τῆς τοῦ πατρὸς ἀπολαύων δυνάμεως. . . .

[6] As Sagnard says (*Les Extraits de Théodote*, Sources Chrétiennes 23, 19 f), "Perhaps if we replace this term 'body' that constrains us (unaccustomed as we are to the continual transpositions of allegory) or even that of 'being' (*ousia*) with that of 'nature,' we could say that the son is 'divine nature.' The son receives his nature from the Father, and cannot be distinguished from him on the basis of this nature, that is to say, on the basis of hypostasis."

very pinnacle of the divine hierarchy (Exc 19.1) .[7] Jn 1.1 and 1.14, far from describing the opposite ends of the range of divine being, Clement claims, actually refer to the *identical* being. In the very delineation of the pre-existent logos from God he can be said to have "become flesh," for his relation to God consists in this process of delineation and not in any diminution of divine being. In the same way, Clement applies Phil 2.6 to the eternal generation of the son from the Father. He calls this generation a "self-emptying," for in the process, he says the son takes a relatively passive and receptive role in relation to the Father as the active, dominant principle (Exc 19.5) .[8] Furthermore, Clement continues, the logos can be said to have "become flesh" again after his generation in the process of becoming creator of the cosmos (Jn 1.3) ; for this reason he is called "firstborn of creation." He has also "become flesh" as he (the logos) was "spoken" through the word of the prophets. Finally he also "becomes flesh" in becoming incarnate as the savior. Lest the Valentinians regard the incarnate savior as a being of lesser divinity than the logos, Clement applies to him the very passage they had reserved for the "highest" divine manifestation— Jn 1.1-3. Stated most simply, what Clement does is to apply to the incarnate savior the passage the Valentinians regarded as "most metaphysical," and to apply the verse they refer to the mere cosmic manifestation in Jesus (Jn 1.14) to the very pre-existent divine logos. Through this technique, Clement ridicules their claim to find in the Johannine prologue evidence of a hierarchically graded structure of divine being. He attempts instead to establish exegetically the claim that "the identical logos-theos" is acting throughout all the manifestations of God to mankind.

Irenaeus' attack

In all probability, Irenaeus is confronted with the same Valentinian source as Clement. He objects first of all to the "method" they use "to subvert scripture, claiming to establish from it their own invention"

[7] Exc 19.1: "καὶ ὁ λόγος σάρξ ἐγένετο," οὐ κατὰ τὴν παρουσίαν μόνον ἄνθρωπος γενόμενος, ἀλλὰ καὶ ἐν ἀρχῇ ὁ ἐν ταυτότητι λόγος, κατὰ περιγραφὴν καὶ οὐ κατ' οὐσίαν γενόμενος υἱός.

[8] Exc 19.5: "His having 'taken the form of a servant' refers not only to his flesh at his coming, but also to his being (*ousia*) which he derived from its underlying reality, for being (*ousia*) is a slave, insofar as it is passive and subordinate to the active and dominating cause."

(AH 1.9.1). He says that exegesis must follow the "clear and open sense of scripture" (AH 2.27.2).[9] He insists, secondly, that interpretation must begin from the "clear and unambiguous parts" of the gospels, as against the Valentinian procedure of first exegeting parables and other metaphorical texts, and taking these as the basis from which to interpret the rest (AH 2.10.1-2). Third, the exegete must attend to the word order and context, without inverting, altering, and segmenting it as the Valentinians do to arrive at their "contrived" exegeses (AH 2.27.1-4).

Irenaeus goes on to say that to refute the Valentinian interpretation of John he merely has to quote their own words, "that you may perceive the perversity of their method and the evil of their error" (AH 1.9.1). In the first place, he argues, had John intended to refer to the pleromic ogdoad, he would have observed the order of the syzygies' emanation. He would have placed the primary tetrad first, and not (as Ptolemy claims it appears in the text) only after the *second* tetrad. Furthermore, he would not have omitted mention of the Ecclesia. Alternatively, if (as Ptolemy claims) the total syzygy were to be inferred from mention of the male member alone, he would have followed this practice with the other syzygies as well. In other words, had that been his intention, the author of John would have presented the ogdoad clearly and consistently—which not even a Valentinian could claim he has done. "Their misuse of exegesis," Irenaeus concludes, "is therefore obvious."

A Valentinian, however, would find the conclusion of this logical argument far from obvious. Most likely he would protest that Irenaeus has missed the point, and therefore has remained unaware of Ptolemy's exegetical skill. Ptolemy himself agrees that from Jn 1.5 the author of the gospel is describing not the ogdoad but the savior's journey outside the pleroma—at least on the *explicit* level of the account. Ptolemy's whole exegetical skill and the measure of his insight (in gnostic terms) is that he is able to perceive and interpret the hidden, implicit level *also* present in the text. It is on this more profound level that John alludes to the ogdoad even as, on the explicit and exoteric level, he is describing other events. Full initiation into gnosis is the essential prerequisite for comprehending such advanced exegesis as Ptolemy presents here. To expect that John would have openly stated such mysteries as that of the primary ogdoad would be simply naïve. As

---

[9] Cf AH 2.27.2: "All scriptures, both the prophets and the gospels, preach openly and without ambiguity (*in aperto et sine ambiguitate*) so that they may be heard in the same way (*similiter*) by all, even if all do not believe."

Irenaeus himself has phrased it, satirizing the Valentinians, they claim "to reveal the most marvelous and profound mysteries, which all are not capable of receiving, because they are not intelligent enough" (AH 1.1). Ptolemy himself has demonstrated in his Letter to Flora that the evident discrepancies in the scriptures cannot be understood apart from a clear understanding of the different levels of divine being, and of how they relate specifically to each exegetical problem.

Irenaeus' claim that valid exegesis must follow the clear and consistent textual wording is alien and contrary to Valentinian epistemology. The presuppositions involved are philosophical and theological. Far from being "self-evident," they form the fundamental issue in this controversy over exegesis.[10] Irenaeus' "refutation" of Valentinian methodology actually consists in a theological counterclaim. He "refutes" their method in terms of his own theological presuppositions. His refutation of Valentinian hermeneutics (as Brox points out[11]) consists in his reasserting the salvation-history theological perspective and the theory of revelation it implies. Irenaeus himself recognizes this, for he aims his next attack on Valentinian exegesis at their *theological* structure, which Clement also attacked.

Irenaeus here presents the cardinal principle of his own exegesis: "that John preaches one God, and one only-begotten son," of whom "all these things [i.e., all the prologue material] are spoken" (AH 1.9.1). The Valentinians, he says, have taken each one of the epithets of Christ and have transferred into them "their own hypothesis." In their view, John does not refer all the epithets to "the Lord Jesus Christ, the teacher of John"; their hypothesis excludes such historical referents. Irenaeus insists that "John the apostle himself has made it clear" that he speaks "not of syzygies but of Jesus Christ." He claims to be able to demonstrate this exegetically from the text.

The crucial text for Irenaeus' "proof" is Jn 1.14. But his very introduction to the text incorporates the theological principle he is claiming to prove. For assuming that the "logos in the archē" is identical to the logos of Jn 1.14, he says that John, "summarizing what he has said above concerning the logos in the archē, explains that this same logos became flesh, and dwelt among us." According to the Valentinian hypothesis, he adds, the logos did not become flesh: "he did not even

---

[10] That von Loewenich (*Johannes-Verständnis*, 120) regards Irenaeus' position as "self-evidently setting forth the basic principles for any sound exegesis" actually amounts to a restatement of his description of Irenaeus as "the founder of orthodox exegesis."

[11] Brox, *Offenbarung*, 69 f; see also 22 f.

come out of the pleroma" (AH 1.9.2). The obvious Valentinian reply would distinguish the Logos of the primary tetrad, who remains within the pleroma, from the logos as savior who emerges beyond it, as well as from the logos "made flesh" in the cosmos. Such a reply would prove wholly unacceptable to Irenaeus, of course, who presupposes that the Christ of history himself is the one logos. Irenaeus goes on to define "flesh" as "the primary element God formed from the earth," in order to exclude by definition the Valentinian savior, "who, they say, put on a psychic body in the oikonomia in order to become visible and tangible" (AH 1.9.3).

Once the full impact of Jn 1.14 is recognized, says Irenaeus (having in mind, of course, the way he himself defines its impact), "their whole hypothesis collapses." He compares them to those who claim to find their own ideas confirmed in the Homeric poems. The chief error in this procedure is that they take phrases out of context and "reassemble them in their own order." Clearly, as noted above, Ptolemy has chosen selectively the verses he exegetes in his prologue commentary. For him, however, the "relevant context" is defined not in terms of simple textual word order, but in terms of the frame of reference (pleromic, kenomic, or cosmic) in which the exegesis operates. Heracleon shares this understanding of "context." For him, as for Ptolemy, "gnosis," and not the textual wording, furnishes the exegetical context.

Irenaeus' methodological critique must give way, then, to a theological one. His most accurate criticism is that the Valentinians, while overtly agreeing with all Christian doctrine, do so on the basis of theological presuppositions fundamentally opposed to those of the majority of Christians. Irenaeus remarks that within the tradition he represents as well there are members of greater and lesser intellectual capacity and theological insight. Those intellectually gifted, however, instead of altering the basis structure (or, to use Irenaeus' term, *hypothesis*) of the common faith, build from it by theological reflection (AH 1.10.2).

The postulate that all "orthodox" Christians hold in common, he continues, proclaims that God is one and his logos is one. It proclaims that the whole revelation of God, insofar as he reveals himself to mankind, is given in creation and in history. From this postulate follows his exegetical principle that all the epithets of the Johannine prologue must refer to the same agent.

Irenaeus' conclusion agrees with Clement's, but his line of reasoning is quite different. Irenaeus repeatedly insists that what man knows of God he knows through creation and the acts of salvation-history alone.

For him neither secret traditions nor metaphysical reflection offer independent means of understanding truth. Had he encountered Clement's doctrine of the distinction between the logos and the savior, he might have accepted it as legitimate theologizing. On the other hand, he might have rejected it as he rejects the Valentinian claim to transcend the manifestations of God in history by teaching "a more elevated and greater God" (AH 1.1). In the same way, he might have had reservations about the metaphysical statements of Jn 1.1-2 themselves, were they not included in so indispensable an authority. He believes that the inclusion of John into the "fourfold gospel" requires that this text conform to what he calls the "catholic interpretation" of the faith.

To understand Irenaeus' hermeneutics, however, one must recognize how he understands the basis of this authority. The only "canon" he explicitly acknowledges is the "canon of truth." This consists (as von Campenhausen points out) neither in a summary of dogmatic statements nor in a formal recognition of "scripture" as such, but in the apprehension of the faith that "the church" has experienced through Christ.[12] The truth lives in "the church" and in its "word." From this point of view, no special documents are necessary (AH 3.4.1).[13] As he engages in controversy with the Marcionites and Valentinians, both claiming the "authority" of authentic written traditions, Irenaeus comes to claim the Pauline corpus and the gospels as a counter-authority from which to refute them.

Irenaeus claims to verify this authority, however, not *formally* but *historically*.[14] It is essential to him that the fourth gospel is, as he says, the witness of "John, the Lord's disciple." His concern is less to establish the validity of the document than the validity of the eyewitness who stands as guarantor to the events there narrated. If the gospel's author can be identified as "the Lord's disciple," this "proves," for him, that the author refers to the Jesus of history and not to syzygies (AH 1.9.1-3).

He offers, then, an allegedly historical account of the gospel's origin, just as for each of the other members of the "four-formed gospel" he documents the author's actual relationship to the Jesus of history (AH 3.1–11.9). John, he says, wrote the gospel to refute the errors of

[12] Von Campenhausen, *Entstehung*, 213.
[13] AH 3.4.1: Even the illiterate Germans, he says, need no *writings* to ensure the faith which the spirit inscribes "on their hearts."
[14] Brox, *Offenbarung*, 76: "The historicizing aspect of scriptural evidence outweighs, for Irenaeus, the theological aspect."

Cerinthus and the Nicolaitans—figures difficult to trace historically, but both traditionally pictured as antagonists of the disciple John.[15] But the "errors" Irenaeus attributes to these figures as the errors John writes to refute, are *Valentinian* doctrines. Having established that the gospel was not only written by the Lord's disciple, but written as a direct anti-gnostic polemic, Irenaeus would secure the validity, indeed, the necessity, of his anti-gnostic interpretation of John. Thereby Irenaeus would show, not from "the text itself," as he had claimed, but from historical grounds, that the Valentinian exegesis is false, and that the interpretation he presents of John, as witness to a historical revelation, is the only valid interpretation.

Just as, in his view, the authenticity of the fourth gospel is historically validated, so also historical events validate the faith itself. For as we have seen, Irenaeus considers these events themselves—and not the evangelistic and apostolic writings that attest them—to be the primary means of revelation. Irenaeus denies that the theological perspective of salvation-history leads to hermeneutical "literalism." It is the Jews, he says, who read their scriptures "literally" when they read them only as a narration of past events, missing the prophetic references to Christ's coming (AH 4.26.1). To read the scriptures accurately requires faith, but certainly not the type of learned exegesis the gnostics contrive. Whoever reads them with faith can recognize that their statements are for the most part clear and self-evident as witnesses to the events of Christ's coming. Their sole and singular meaning is to proclaim and to witness to him.

The hermeneutical correlate of this salvation-history perspective is historical typology. To explicate the texts, one must simply demonstrate the typological correlation between the ancient prophecies and the events that fulfill them. As Irenaeus says, every detail of Christ's coming was predicted and well known in advance. Before his incarnation, however, the prophecies remained incomprehensible. "Every prophecy, before its fulfillment, remains an enigma and a contradiction; but when the time comes and the prophesied event occurs, then it has a whole and specific interpretation" (AH 4.26.1).

The exegete's task, then, is to perceive and interpret this correlation of prophecy to fulfillment, of prototypical event to the "event itself." Irenaeus interprets "scripture" as a whole, then, typologically. He also interprets some sections allegorically. Irenaeus does not oppose the use of allegory *per se:* he himself uses it as a means of expounding

[15] On Cerinthus, see the summary of evidence in von Loewenich, *Johannes-Verständnis,* 62. The Nicolaitans are denounced by "John" in Rev 2.6.

obscure passages. What he rejects is the theological premise that underlies gnostic allogorizing—the premise that the events related in the
gospels are meaningless until they are interpreted allegorically. What
he considers crucial is not the specific method one uses, but that one
approach exegesis from the theological perspective of salvation-history.

Irenaeus perceives that this whole theological approach is at issue
in the controversy with the Valentinians. While they claim to accept
the "historical level" of Christian teaching, they reject its basic premise:
that events given in and through history are the primary medium of
revelation. For them such events remain, at best, a mere indication,
a hint of realities that transcend space and time.

The centrality of this theological issue explains why methodological
criticism of Valentinian exegesis, both ancient and modern, remains,
even when valid, largely irrelevant. Irenaeus himself often quotes
verses from the gospels selectively and out of context, as he accuses
Ptolemy of doing. He also uses allegorical forms of exegesis for which he
castigates the gnostics.[16] As for "that well-known feature of Valentinian exegesis, (a) minute attention to grammatical detail . . . which
often leads to an overstraining of language," [17] such attention to
minutiae characterizes the Alexandrian fathers' exegesis as well.
Where, conversely, Valentinian exegetes are credited by modern
scholars as being more textually acute or more historically sound than
their "orthodox" counterparts,[18] here again, theological considerations
often dictate the exegetical practice of both commentators.

The characteristically Valentinian exegetical practices, such as their
selective use of passages to fit into the framework of the exegesis, the
hypostasization of nouns, and their interpretation of events as symbols
of spiritual processes can be shown, likewise, to derive from their
theological outlook.

Heracleon on the prologue

Irenaeus might have been harder pressed to make such a case against
Heracleon—that Valentinian theologian who was apparently his con-

[16] Brox, *Offenbarung*, 85 f: AH 5.33.4. Irenaeus explains here that some passages do offer "double meanings." To these he also applies allegorical interpretation. As Gögler says (*Theologie*, 108) : "Irenaeus explains the whole of scripture
typologically, and part of it allegorically . . . . The problem for Irenaeus is not the
question of whether scripture is exegeted correctly typologically or allegorically, but
what rule may prevent it from being used arbitrarily according to the gnostic way."

[17] Sanders, *Fourth Gospel*, 62.

[18] Cf Brooke, *Fragments*, 47; W. Förster, *Von Valentin zu Heracleon* (Giessen,
1928) , 5; Loewenich, *Johannes-Verständnis*, 87.

temporary. Reference to the pleroma or to the mythic drama of Sophia is virtually absent from the extant fragments of Heracleon's exegesis. His interpretation of the Johannine prologue, so far as it is available, begins with Jn 1.3. Heracleon, like Irenaeus himself, refers this verse to the creation of "the cosmos and everything in it." Did Heracleon begin his commentary with exegesis of Jn 1.1-2? The theological structure of Origen's discussion of these verses indicates that Origen directs his argument against such exegesis as Ptolemy's. Throughout the two volumes he devotes to this material, Origen (contrary to his frequent practice) neither mentions nor attacks any position of Heracleon. It is quite possible, of course, that Heracleon did write an exegesis of this passage which is now lost.

On the other hand, if Heracleon deliberately has *omitted* these two verses from his commentary, we may suggest a hypothesis to account for such an omission. In this case his selection of material for exegesis (like Ptolemy's, see above, p. 32) may be guided by his choice of an exegetical framework. Having decided, apparently, to interpret the gospel in terms of the *cosmic* context, Heracleon may not have considered the two opening verses (which describe what has occurred *prior to* the creation of the cosmos) to be appropriate for this exegetical context. That the extant fragments begin, then, with verse 3, the verse describing the cosmic creation, may not be due to historical accident. In any case, as noted already, Heracleon interprets the "all things" of Jn 1.3 as "the cosmos and its contents" (CJ 2.14).

Heracleon says that, conversely, the statement that "apart from him nothing came into being" means "nothing of what is in the cosmos and in creation." He claims the right to make this addition by referring to the traditions of Valentinian exegesis. But he goes on to offer an exegesis that seems, at first glance, so uncharacteristic of Valentinian theology that de Faye has concluded that Heracleon is no traditional Valentinian at all, but a theological revisionist, who offers in place of the older myth a "strictly monotheist" and "christianized" theology.[19] For Heracleon specifies that the aion (*plērōma*) and its contents have not come into being through the logos, but that the pleroma has originated "before" the logos. The creation of the cosmos, he adds, is the work of the logos himself.

Yet Heracleon's interpretation of "all things," despite the superficial similarity with Irenaeus' doctrine that has led some scholars to equate the two exegeses, remains very far from it. Irenaeus always insists that

[19] *Gnostiques,* 53. See also above, p. 25, n. 8, for citations from scholars who share de Faye's view.

"from *all things* nothing is excluded" (AH 1.22.1). In his view, as we have seen, the term loses its meaning if anything in creation is excluded from it. For Heracleon, on the other hand (as Origen points out), the term is more exclusive than inclusive. Granted, he does refer it to the cosmos and its contents. But he "leaves out of the *all things,* according to his hypothesis, everything *not* included in the cosmos, by which he means the pleroma." As Origen says, "he excludes from this precisely what he considers divine, and what he regards as wholly corruptible is what he calls *all things"* (CJ 2.14). The precise and limited scope Heracleon designates for the referent of the "all things" —that it means only the world and its contents—corresponds to the precisely limited scope he intends his exegesis of the verse to offer. His exegesis operates not in terms of the *pleroma* nor of the *kenoma* but specifically in terms of the *cosmos.*

In the same way he defines the logos to whom his exegesis refers as that logos who comes into existence *after* the pleroma. He says elsewhere that "the logos is the savior" (CJ 6.20), the savior who comes "out of the aion." The creator "is Christ," since "all things were made by him, and without him nothing was made" (CJ 13.19). He takes care to specify that when he speaks of logos he is referring neither to the pleromic aion nor to the kenomic Christ, but to the logos who manifests himself as creator of the cosmos and as the savior.

When he considers the words of Jn 1.4, that "what came to be in him was life," Heracleon again interprets this verse, as noted above, in terms of the cosmic manifestation of the "life." In this context, the phrase "in him" means "in those human beings who are pneumatic" (CJ 2.21). Heracleon thereby indicates that this "life" cannot be taken in a literal sense to refer to the animate life of all mankind; it refers to the savior and the divine life he offers. Secondly, he indicates that this "life" emerges not in all human beings, but only in certain ones. Third, he indicates that those in whom the "life" emerges, the "pneumatics," stand in a special relation to the logos. The theological problem that emerges here is the problem of how human beings are related to the "life": who receives it, and by what process? Origen, aware of this problem, attacks Heracleon's exegesis here as "forced" and "violent." He accuses Heracleon of considering "the logos and the pneumatics to be identical, even if he has not said this clearly." He points out that Heracleon "as if explaining this, says, 'he (the logos) provided them with their first form according to origin (*genesis*), bringing and manifesting what had been sown by another into form and enlightenment and into its own definition" (CJ 2.21). According

48

to Origen, Heracleon is propounding a deterministic theory of salvation, a theory that there are "spiritual natures" (*physeis pneumatikas*) which are so "from birth"; and that this divine "life" emerges in these alone (CJ 2.20). Conversely, Origen continues, this theory maintains that others are "lost natures," lost from birth. These have no possibility of sharing in the "life." For this "hypothesis about different natures" (which Origen interprets as a substantive determinism), he says Heracleon offers no proof at all, which demonstrates his inability to defend such a view. With this, Origen dismisses the matter.

His interpretation of Heracleon's soteriology as substantive determinism enables Origen summarily to dismiss the Valentinian viewpoint as indefensible and implausible. For the purpose of his polemic —of protecting believers from "heterodox" opinions—he succeeds in reducing the Valentinian position to absurdity. Yet he has succeeded, one might say, too well. He has not only put forth a deft caricature of their position, but he has succeeded in convincing many scholars as well, whose intention is not (avowedly, at least) polemical but historical, to accept this caricature of the Valentinian position as an accurate description of it.

Origen did not originate such an interpretation of Valentinian soteriology. Clement of Alexandria, Irenaeus, and other anti-Valentinian writers before him made the same accusation. In Origen's time, however, the problem of "the natures"—the question of anthropology (and hence of soteriology)—has become the central issue of the anti-Valentinian controversy. Hippolytus and Irenaeus, who often focus their attack on the Valentinians' "extravagant mythology," concern themselves to a greater extent with the metaphysical structure which is mythologically expressed. Clement, attacking their metaphysical system, directs his polemic primarily against Ptolemy's prologue exegesis. Origen, who selects for attack Heracleon's exegesis of John, has chosen to refute a work primarily concerned with soteriology. Although he draws on stock arguments of his predecessors against Valentinian "mythopoetics," he centers his attack on their anthropological theory, which he calls their "doctrine of natures." Our examination of Heracleon's exegesis, then, must examine the presuppositions of his exegetical comments on soteriology.

Further evidence of Heracleon's prologue exegesis is almost entirely missing. It was included, apparently, in the missing third volume of Origen's commentary. The catena fragments of Origen's exegesis offer, however, hints of Heracleon's exegesis. Apparently Heracleon has referred Jn 1.8, which states that the baptist "was not the light," to the demiurge (CJ Frag 6). From Origen's discussion of Jn 1.12 we infer that Heracleon has distinguished between two different responses to the savior encountered in the cosmos. First, there are those who "received him," to whom he gave "power to become the sons of God." Second (and distinct from these) are those who "believe on his name" (CJ Frag 7). Further investigation will show how this distinction concurs with Heracleon's distinction between the pneumatic and psychic experience of the savior—the pneumatics being those who "become sons of God," and the psychics those who only "believe on his name." Origen's argument supports this inference when he claims that the two phrases must refer to the same persons. At Jn 1.14, he argues that the term *monogenēs* can be taken only in the singular, and that it signifies the uniqueness of Christ in comparison with all other beings (CJ Frag 9). Heracleon, we surmise, consistent with his interpretation of 1.4, may have taken this pluralistically to include the "pneumatics" who have become "sons of God" as essentially identical with the savior.

The lacunae in the text require us to turn next to the discussion of John the baptist presented in Origen's sixth volume, where Heracleon expounds more clearly his soteriological theory.

3. John the Baptist (Jn 1.19-34) in Valentinian Exegesis

Heracleon's interpretation of John the baptist has served his commentators—from Origen to Sagnard—as evidence for his "theory of natures." Consequently this section offers a crucial place to begin investigation of Heracleon's soteriology.

Origen's argument, as noted above, indicates that Heracleon has interpreted Jn 1.7-8 (the saying that John came to "bear witness to the light," and that he was "not the light" himself) as a reference to the demiurge. According to Heracleon, the demiurge is devoid of "light," that is, of the pneumatic "life" which the savior shares with the pneumatics. Passages from Heracleon's exegesis in Origen's sixth volume confirm these inferences. According to the fragments preserved there, Heracleon first mentions the baptist in his discussion of Jn 1.16-18 (CJ 6.3). The baptist, he says, witnesses in 1.16 that he has "received from the fullness (*plērōma*) of Christ grace upon grace." Heracleon concludes that the following testimony of 1.18 ("no one has ever seen the father") could not have been said by the baptist (i.e., by the demiurge).

Heracleon does not base his argument on text-critical grounds, as A. E. Brooke supposed.[1] Instead, stating explicitly that the baptist rep-

---

[1] Brooke (*Fragments*, 47) praises Heracleon's textual observation over Origen's at this point, calling him "an acute and accurate observer."

resents the demiurge, he infers that the demiurge, who lacks the pneumatic "life," could bear only a limited testimony to Christ. He is able to recognize that the savior is "before" himself (1.16). He can also claim to have received spiritual gifts from the pleroma of the savior (1.17), acknowledging that the law given "through Moses" (that is, through the demiurge himself) has been surpassed by the "grace and truth (*charis* and *alētheia*)" which have come "through Christ." Yet the demiurge could not have uttered the testimony of 1.18, for only at the pneumatic level could one perceive that "the Father is invisible," and only the pneumatic could testify to the Monogenes in the pleroma. With this reasoning, Heracleon therefore ascribes 1.18 to the gospel writer John, whose conception, unlike the baptist's (i.e., the demiurge's), was certainly on the pneumatic level.

Three levels of interpretation

Heracleon, following Valentinian tradition, applies the metaphysical principle of the three ontological levels of being hermeneutically, discerning in the gospel three distinct levels of exegesis. Visible, historical events perceived through the senses occur at the hylic level; the ethical interpretation of these events is perceived as the psychic level; and true insight (*gnōsis*) into them is perceived only at the pneumatic level (see also Origen, below, p. 111). Whoever understands the text pneumatically, then, transcends the mere historical level, and transcends as well its ethical meaning. He comes to interpret the whole symbolically.

When Heracleon considers the figure of John the baptist, then, he regards him not as a historical person primarily but as a symbol—in this case, as a symbol of the demiurge (CJ 3.69). Bethany, where John baptizes, similarly is not to be taken literally as the designation of a geographical place, but is to be interpreted as a "place" in a symbolic sense. Heracleon analyzes, in fact, the whole Johannine topography symbolically. He claims that all the "places" (*topoi*) mentioned represent different "places" where men stand in relation to the revelation in Christ. Their relative elevations signify lower and higher levels of spiritual insight. Capernaum, for example, a low-lying region "near the sea" (CJ 13.60), signifies "those extremities of the cosmos, the hylic regions" (CJ 10.11), while Bethany, where the baptist works, signifies a higher, yet still intermediate region. Jerusalem, higher still, represents the "psychic topos" (CJ 10.33). The "holy of holies" of the

Jerusalem temple, situated at the highest point in the city, signifies the "pneumatic topos." In this way the *topoi* become a fundamental metaphor for the different "levels" of spiritual insight, and the different "standpoints" of men in relation to the revelation.

This interplay between the literal level of the text, the ethical interpretation, and the spiritual or symbolic interpretation characterizes Heracleon's whole conception of exegesis. He sees the discerning of these levels not only as his own hermeneutical task, but also as the activity of the persons described *within* the text. It is not only Heracleon himself, as exegete, but also those persons described in the accounts who, according to the three levels of perception, must interpret who "John the baptist" really is.

According to the account, the baptist appears "in his externality," at least, as a "prophet." In terms of the expectation of those who surround him, he is a prophet. Heracleon explains that, as such, the baptist participates in the "prophetic order" which functions entirely within the region (*topos*) of sense-perception. Alternatively, this region can be called metaphorically the region of "sound," for it consists of purely sensible utterance (CJ 6.20). The priests and levites of Israel, themselves standing at the "region" of sense-perception, come to John asking who he is. They can perceive only his "externality" which is accessible to sense-perception. When John replies to their questions that he is "not a prophet," Heracleon explains that he is refusing to answer their question as they intended it—on an external and sensible level alone (CJ 6.30). Their attempt to identify John with his external appearance, Heracleon says, is like trying to identify a person with the clothes he wears. Someone who is asked "if he were himself his clothes, could not say yes!"

Heracleon then explains the apparent contradiction in the text between what John says of himself—that he is *not* a prophet, nor Elijah —and what the savior says of John—that he *is* a prophet, and Elijah (Jn 1.21; Mt 11.13-14). When the savior calls John a prophet, "he speaks not of John himself but of his externality." When, on the other hand, John insists he is not a prophet, and the savior himself says John is "greater than a prophet," then, Heracleon says, John is characterized not in terms of his externality, but in terms of his interiority: it is "John himself" that is so characterized.[2]

---

[2] CJ 6. (20.) 112: καὶ προφήτην μὲν καὶ Ἡλίαν ὁ σωτὴρ ἐπὰν αὐτὸν λέγῃ, οὐκ αὐτὸν ἀλλὰ τὰ περὶ αὐτόν, φησί, διδάσκει· ὅταν δὲ μείζονα προφητῶν καὶ ἐν γεννητοῖς γυναικῶν, τότε αὐτὸν τὸν Ἰωάννην χαρακτηρίζει αὐτὸς δέ, φησί, περὶ ἑαυτοῦ ἐρωτώμενος ἀποκρίνεται ὁ Ἰωάννης, οὐ τὰ περὶ αὐτόν . . . .

What appears as a contradiction is actually, Heracleon explains, a paradox intended to differentiate between two levels of perceiving John and his activity. According to the lower, external level, John is a prophet, and belongs to the prophetic order of sense-perception alone. Yet John "himself" who formerly belonged to that prophetic order, has now received from Christ's pleroma an additional grace beyond that of the prophets (Jn 1.16). This grace enables him to perceive that the law has now been surpassed in Christ's revelation. This higher level of insight reconstitutes John in his inner selfhood: "he himself" no longer belongs only to the old order, and therefore he denies that "he himself" is a prophet. Inwardly he is "greater than Elijah and all the prophets." His distinction above them is marked in that his coming was itself predicted by the prophet Isaiah, as that of the "voice crying in the wilderness" (CJ 6.21).

Heracleon then sets forth the relation of the three levels or "standpoints" of perception in the following metaphor:

The logos is the savior; the voice (phonē), what John interpreted in the wilderness; the sound (ēchos), the whole prophetic order.

The voice, being more akin to logos, becomes logos, as also the woman is changed into a man.

The sound can be changed into voice; the voice which is transformed into logos is given the position of a disciple, while sound transformed into voice is given that of a servant.[3]

John, who previously belonged to the "prophetic order" of sound, that is, purely sensible utterance, is that "sound which has been transformed into voice." The purely sense-perceptible has now become utterance that, through sense-perceptible means, now conveys rational meaning. As "sound transformed into voice," he has now attained the position of "servant." For this reason, Heracleon explains, the demiurge, represented as John, confesses that he is the "forerunner" and "servant" of the savior, "unworthy to perform for him the least service." Having gained this level of insight, however, the demiurge still remains limited. He admits his incapacity to understand the "mysteries" of Christ's manifestation (CJ 6.39). In terms of Valentinian analysis, his apprehension, once hylic, wholly "sensible," has now become psychic.

[3] CJ 6. (20.) 108, 111: Ὁ λόγος μὲν ὁ σωτήρ ἐστιν, φωνὴ δὲ ἡ ἐν τῇ ἐρήμῳ ἡ διὰ Ἰωάννου διανοουμένη, ἦχος δὲ πᾶσα προφητικὴ τάξις. . .
τῷ ἤχῳ φησὶν ἔσεσθαι τὴν εἰς φωνὴν μεταβολήν, μαθητοῦ μὲν χώραν διδοὺς τῇ μεταβαλλούσῃ εἰς λόγον φωνῇ, δούλου δὲ τῇ ἀπὸ ἤχου εἰς φωνήν.

The second part of the metaphor refers to a higher stage of trans-formation inaccessible to the demiurge. This involves the transforma-tion from the intermediate, psychic level of insight to its highest, pneu-matic fulfillment. In the process of this transformation, the "woman is changed into a man," the servant becomes a disciple, the voice be-comes logos.

How are we to interpret the distinctions Heracleon draws between hylic, psychic, and pneumatic "levels" of apprehension? Origen claims that the meaning is quite clear—Heracleon teaches a doctrine of "natures," alleging that the differences men experience in levels of spiritual insight derive from predetermined "natures." Sagnard also has recently restated the claim that Heracleon's exegesis of John the baptist presupposes an anthropological theory of "natures." The duality in John consists, according to Sagnard, in his being, "as prophet," of "psychic nature." Indeed, says Sagnard, "he symbolizes the principle of this psychic substance." Insofar as he is "more than prophet," Sagnard continues, he is of "pneumatic nature." Consistent with this interpretation, Sagnard, considering the sound/voice/logos saying, concludes that "voice" is equivalent to the "pneumatic nature," symbolized by John the baptist. "Sound," then, is the "psychic nature," symbolized by the prophets.[4]

The first difficulty with this view is that Heracleon never applies the attributes of the "natures" either to the baptist or to the terms sound/voice/logos. Secondly, Sagnard's view that the baptist's higher "nature" is pneumatic contradicts Heracleon's specific statements that even in his role as voice (which Sagnard takes to mean pneumatic) the bap-tist is excluded from the higher secrets of gnosis. Although he an-nounces the new *oikonomia*, he cannot testify in 1.18 to the "gnosis of the father." Although he serves and heralds Christ, he confesses that he cannot "understand or explain" the *oikonomia* of the new revelation. The third difficulty with Sagnard's theory is that the sound/voice/logos saying is a metaphor of transformation, which cannot apply to the natures. Sagnard himself criticizes Henrici for failing to recognize that the natures, being "unalterable," cannot be transformed into each other. Henrici, he says, misunderstands the gnostic principle:

[4] Sagnard, *Gnose:* "John the baptist, being simultaneously 'prophet' and 'more than prophet,' that is, pneumatic nature enveloped in psychic . . . is the perfect gnostic personification, since he is double . . ." (493). "As prophet, that is, psychic, he symbolizes the head of this psychic substance" (513). Sagnard divides his dis-cussion (513-514), entitled "John the baptist, double personification," into the two sections, 1. "John the baptist, the prophet (psychic)," and 2. "John the baptist, more than prophet (pneumatic)."

Nothing psychic enters into the pleroma. It is a matter of structure: what is psychic will remain always at the door of the pleroma, outside of the pneumatic sphere.[5]

If then, the three stages described in the metaphor as sound/voice/logos cannot be regarded as simply equivalent to the three natures, how are we to understand their relation to the theory of natures? The metaphor itself suggests the answer. These are stages in a process of *transformation in gnosis,* stages which can be described in the alternate metaphors of sound/voice/logos, woman/man, servant/disciple. John the baptist exemplifies the transition from sound to voice, which is the transition from ignorance of the highest God to a median stage of gnosis where he can perceive the difference between the two *oikonomiai.* But he cannot progress through the second level of transformation—to the level of the highest gnosis. In the language of the metaphor, as the sound become voice, he has become the servant of the revelation; but he has not passed from voice to logos, from the position of servant to that of disciple.

As the terms of the sayings are stages of transformation in gnosis, the baptist exemplifies the person who stands at the *psychic* stage (*topos*). John, who has "ascended" from the hylic topos to the psychic, expresses that median level of gnosis accessible at the psychic level. Noting that Jn 10.40 speaks of the "topos" where John baptizes, Heracleon points out that this topos extends from the lower, hylic region of Capernaum to the city of Jerusalem (CJ 10.33). Capernaum, as he has explained, symbolizes the spiritual condition of total ignorance, the topos, or standpoint, of the hylics; while Jerusalem symbolizes the median, or psychic, level of insight. He shows, then, in this geographical metaphor the range of insight (*gnōsis*) accessible within this "region." As the baptist moves precisely within this range, his words and actions epitomize this median level of gnosis.

The higher, spiritual topos, represented as the "holy of holies," remains beyond the psychic topos, inaccessible to John the baptist. The higher transformation from voice into logos, from servant into disciple, from woman into man, then, is the transformation from the *psychic* into the *pneumatic* topos. It is the Samaritan woman of Jn 4 who exemplifies this transformation as she passes from ignorance of the higher God into the fullness of gnosis. This process we shall examine below in chapter five. For present purposes, it suffices to see

[5] *Gnose,* 492-493, 361-362.

56

how the baptist exemplifies the level of gnosis available at the psychic topos.

Instead of a static and deterministic "theory of natures," I would suggest that Heracleon is setting forth a theory of the dynamic transformation of human insight. Through his exegesis of the baptist, he offers an analysis of three distinct "levels" of such insight, ranging from the "hylic," that is, from merely sense-perceptible perception devoid of spiritual content, through a median, "psychic" level, to the "pneumatic" level of symbolic understanding. This is not to say (as Langerbeck and Schottroff have claimed[6]) that all three "levels" are accessible to all men alike. The question of access to these three levels has yet to be considered.

Heracleon's criticism of non-Valentinian baptism

In offering this analysis, Heracleon does not intend merely to construct a theoretical anthropology. The fragments of his commentary indicate that he writes it not only to exegete the gospel, but also to use exegesis as a means of criticizing specific conceptions and practices of certain Christians. These, apparently, are Christian groups he knows in Alexandria at the time of his activity there (*ca.* 160-180). He writes to urge those who are capable to seek a higher level of insight (*gnōsis*). He intends his characterization of the baptist and the "psychic level" of insight as a description of what he considered to be a common "standpoint" of many Christians in relation to the revelation in Christ. He considers this standpoint not as directly wrong, but as distinctly limited, and cut off from a higher apprehension of Christ.

What we know historically of Heracleon's actual situation is, as scholars have recognized, extremely limited. Harnack has stated that "the most serious lack in our knowledge of the early church is our almost total ignorance of the history of Christianity in Alexandria and Egypt . . . up to the year 180 (Demetrius' episcopate)." [7] W. Bauer, examining the evidence available to him (*ca.* 1934), appraises the sources even more critically than Harnack. Bauer questions Harnack's representation of Barnabas as a witness to "orthodox" Chris-

---

[6] H. Langerbeck, *Aufsätze zur Gnosis* (Göttingen, 1967); L. Schottroff "Animae naturaliter salvandae," in *Christentum und Gnosis,* ed. W. Eltester (Berlin, 1969), 65 f.

[7] A. Harnack, *The Mission and Expansion of Christianity in the First Three Centuries* 2 (transl. by J. Moffatt from the 2nd German edition of 1906; London, 1908), 158.

tianity in Alexandria, and suggests that the bishops' lists which begin from the year 189 refer only to certain groups of Alexandrian Christians. He observes that evidence of other Christian groups is offered in such Coptic-gnostic writings as the Apocryphon of John, Pistis Sophia, and the Odes of Solomon, and that such gnostic teachers as Basilides, Carpocrates, Valentinus, and Isidore are known to have been active at that period.[8] Since the time of his writing, of course, the discoveries at Nag Hammadi have opened up new and greatly extended areas of research into the early history of Christianity in Egypt. Puech and Quispel have even suggested that one of the Nag Hammadi manuscripts, the so-called Treatise on Three Natures, may be the work of Heracleon himself.[9]

It is now generally recognized that at the time of Heracleon's activity in Alexandria, the boundaries of what later came to be called "orthodoxy" and "heresy" were not fixed. The necessity of distinguishing the "true meaning of Christianity" from false or superficial understandings of it, and of defining true Christian worship over against erroneous forms of worship, concerned the Valentinians at least as much as it concerned those who identified themselves with the emerging mainstream of Christianity. When Clement "set himself the task of explaining what is inmost and highest in Christianity," [10] he must have recognized the Valentinian theologians, like Ptolemy and Heracleon, as his predecessors in this endeavor. But Clement (as Harnack points out) strives continually "to preserve his connection to the main body of Christendom." [11] Heracleon, on the other hand, seeks to define the inner and true interpretation of the faith over against "the many," whose beliefs and practices, he claims, are not only limited, as Clement readily admits, but also misleading and erroneous.

The hypothesis that Heracleon intends his exegesis of John the baptist to characterize the "standpoint" of "the many" Christians receives support in Heracleon's discussion of the relation between the "levels" of perception and three distinct "levels" of baptism. For the "hylic" and "psychic" levels of baptism, as he describes them, correspond strikingly to what we know of the baptismal theology and practice of the second-century Christian "mainstream." Investigation of his

[8] *Orthodoxy and Heresy in Earliest Christianity* (transl. and ed. by R. Kraft and G. Krodel from the 2nd German edition of 1964; Philadelphia, 1971) , 44-60.

[9] H.-C. Puech and G. Quispel, "Le Quatrième Ecrit Gnostique du Codex Jung," Vigiliae Christianae 9 (1955) , 65 f.

[10] A. Harnack, *History of Dogma* 2.6 (transl. and ed. by N. Buchanan from the German edition of 1894; reprinted New York, 1961) , 326.

[11] *Dogma* 2.6, 327.

view of baptism may serve to define more precisely not only his own theological intention, but also that of "the many" whom he criticizes.

In discussing the baptist, Heracleon explains that only the representatives of the lowest, "prophetic order" have "the duty of baptizing" (CJ 6.23). At this level, which is bounded by sense-perception, baptism consists of a merely physical act—the bodily washing "with water." John, in his "external" and historical role, does baptize. Yet inwardly, "he himself" does *not* baptize.[12] As "voice" he offers not the physical act but its interior, ethical meaning, which is "repentance" and "forgiveness of sins."

The levites who question John, seeing only what their senses perceive, see that John baptizes with water, and ascribe this to his role as they see it—as prophet. They do not understand his insistence that "he himself" does *not* baptize. They fail to realize that, in saying this, he refers to his own interior being. Again what seems at the literal level to be a contradiction is actually a paradox—this time intended to differentiate between two levels of perceiving John's baptizing. The first level is "somatic," and sees the act only as an external washing with water. The second is "psychic," and perceives the inner "repentance and forgiveness" conveyed in and through the physical act.

John himself, however, proclaims the coming of one "greater than" himself, who will come after him and offer a baptism greater than his own—the baptism of the "holy spirit" (Jn 1.33). This one, of course, is Christ, the savior. He alone can offer the third and higher aspect of baptism, which conveys the spirit. As John operates on the somatic level, metaphorically called "sound," and on the psychic level, called "voice," the savior operates on the spiritual level as well, that of "logos." The savior himself encompasses all three levels. So John, as "prophet," points out the savior's physical presence when he announces the "lamb of God," which, as Heracleon explains, signifies "the body" of Jesus. As "more than prophet," John speaks on the psychic level, proclaiming the "one in the body," the psychic Christ who "takes away the sins of the world" (CJ 6.60). In a higher, spiritual sense, however, the savior is "already present in the cosmos and in men" (CJ 6.38) as their spiritual "life." Yet this spiritual presence is not manifest to all, not even to John, whose utterances remain on the somatic and

---

[12] Origen places Heracleon's argument in the mouth of the Pharisees, whom he sees as hostile and arrogant: "Their mission is sent to prevent the baptist from baptizing, as if it were thought that no one were 'entitled to baptize but Christ and Elijah and the prophet'" (CJ 6.8).

psychic levels alone. "Spiritually the savior is present only in those human beings who are spiritual."

Through the figure of John, Heracleon explains, the demiurge acknowledges that the prophetic order of "sound" has ended; and he himself, as "voice," announces the advent of the psychic order. Yet he recognizes that he can only grasp the meaning of Christ's coming *psychically,* being unable to apprehend its full, *spiritual* significance:

I am not worthy that he should descend, for my sake, from the greatness, and take flesh as his sandal—I cannot give account of this, nor interpret nor explain this *oikonomia*.[13]

Remaining as he does on the psychic level, the demiurge can only glimpse Christ's coming and prepare others for it by administering the somatic and psychic baptism.

Who are those who receive his baptism—the "baptism of John," which means, in Valentinian terms, the baptism of the demiurge? The Valentinians, as noted above, characterize the demiurge as the God whom the "psychic Christians" worship as their God. Those who worship the creator and father of the (psychic) Christ are, in Valentinian analysis, lost and immersed in sins until they come to believe in Christ's power of forgiveness. When they repent, it is they who receive the "baptism of John," that is, of the demiurge.

The baptism they practice, however, does not convey the "spirit" which the "spiritual" alone receive. This higher baptism "of Christ" has nothing to do with either the physical washing or the psychic cleansing from sins. Instead it "perfects the spirit" in those who are the elect. Heracleon's discussion of Christ's baptism is missing from the extant fragments. But Irenaeus' description of Valentinian baptismal theology offers an illuminating parallel: "The *baptism* of the visible Jesus, on the one hand, is for the remission of sins; but the *redemption* of the Christ who descends on him is for perfection. The first is *psychic,* the second *pneumatic.* For the baptizing of John is preached for *repentance;* but the redemption of the Christ who is in Jesus is ordained for *perfection.*"[14] This, the explanation continues, is why Jesus, being

---

[13] CJ 6.39: Οὐκ ἐγώ εἰμι ἱκανός, ἵνα δι' ἐμὲ κατέλθῃ ἀπὸ μεγέθους καὶ σάρκα λάβῃ ὡς ὑπόδημα, περὶ ἧς ἐγὼ λόγον ἀποδοῦναι οὐ δύναμαι οὐδὲ διηγήσασθαι ἢ ἐπιλῦσαι τὴν περὶ αὐτῆς οἰκονομίαν.

[14] AH 1.21.2: τὸ μὲν γὰρ βάπτισμα τοῦ φαινομένου ᾽Ιησοῦ ἀφέσεως <εῖναι> ἁμαρτιῶν, τὴν δὲ ἀπολύτρωσιν τοῦ ἐν αὐτῷ Χριστοῦ κατελθόντος εἰς τελείωσιν, καὶ τὸ μὲν ψυχικόν, τὴν δὲ πνευματικὴν εῖναι ὑφίστανται, καὶ τὸ μὲν βάπτισμα ὑπὸ ᾽Ιωάννου κατηγγέλθαι εἰς μετάνοιαν, τὴν δὲ ἀπολύτρωσιν ὑπὸ Χριστοῦ κεκομίσθαι εἰς τελείωσιν.

baptized somatically and psychically by John, speaks of "another baptism" he must yet receive (Mt 10.38; Lk 12.50). Shortly thereafter, a threefold distinction is given. The "redemption" is not corporeal, for the body perishes, nor is it psychic, since the soul comes from a lesser creation: the redemption is therefore pneumatic (AH 1.21.4).

John, then, baptizes "with water" in his externality, as "prophet." In his interiority, he does not physically baptize, but offers the "baptism of repentance for the forgiveness of sins," that belongs to the psychic order. But John can offer only these two levels of baptism. He cannot offer the third, pneumatic level. The savior, however, offers baptism on all three levels. In his external, bodily aspect, he baptizes "with water"; as the psychic son of the demiurge, he offers the baptism "of repentance"; and finally, as the savior who receives the *pneuma Christou* he offers the third baptism, the "redemption." This is pneumatic, conveys the spirit, and is rendered "for perfection." As it consists of initiation into the highest gnosis, this is accessible only to the elect.

From Heracleon's exegesis, then, emerges a theological critique of the sacrament of baptism practiced by "psychic" Christians. Their baptism is, from his viewpoint, "somatic," in that it is a physical act performed on the body. In its interior aspect, it may attain to the psychic level, which consists of repentance and forgiveness. Such a baptism corresponds to Heracleon's conception of psychics as bound to a median and ethical way of attaining salvation "through works" (CJ 13.60). Irenaeus recognizes that this Valentinian distinction between psychic baptism and spiritual "redemption" devalues the meaning and effect of the church's sacrament. This doctrine, he says, was introduced by Satan to negate "the baptism of regeneration unto God" and to destroy "the whole faith" (AH 1.21.1). Irenaeus claims (as Justin and others had before him) that the church's baptism conveys not only the forgiveness of sins, but also such "spiritual gifts" as "illumination" and "regeneration." The Valentinian critique of the church's baptism, which denies to it these spiritual gifts, does focus on what was apparently the most generally accepted view in the second-century church. For, as Harnack says,

since the middle of the second century, the notions of baptism have not essentially altered. The result of baptism was universally considered to be forgiveness of sins, and this pardon was supposed to effect an actual sinlessness which now required to be maintained.[15]

[15] *Dogma* 2.3, 140.

The Valentinian sacrament of "apolytrosis"

Of what, then, does the "spiritual baptism" of "redemption" (*apoly-trōsis*) consist? Can we discover in the formulae Irenaeus cites evidence that concurs with Heracleon's statements, in order to define its efficacy more precisely? Irenaeus first mentions the sacrament of *apolytrōsis* in relation to the circle of Marcus, who is said to be a follower of Valentinus (AH 1.13.1). These gnostics claim, he says, to have become "perfect," to have received gnosis of "the ineffable power," and to have been freed from all the "powers" of the demiurge: ". . . for they claim that because of the *apolytrōsis* they neither can be apprehended nor perceived by the judge (*kritēs*)" (AH 1.13.6). The formula Irenaeus cites in 1.13.6 consists of an appeal to the Mother, the "companion of God, mystic Sige who is before the aion," and who is the higher source of creation, "through whom the angels behold the presence of the Father." The initiates pray to her as being her offspring, who have emerged as "images" of the aions "through the goodness of the Primal Father (*propatēr*)." They invoke her to defend them, as her own, from the "judge." She knows, they say, which are subject to his jurisdiction (apparently psychics) and which are not: they ask her to manifest their identity with her, and thereby to exempt them from his judgment.

In the extant fragments of Heracleon's commentary on John we find no explicit *apolytrōsis* formulae. Exegeting Jn 8.50, however, he does refer to the demiurge as the judge (*kritēs*) whom he represents here in his function as "lawgiver," as Moses (CJ 20.38). It is he who "seeks and judges, being the servant appointed for this purpose, who 'does not bear the sword in vain.'" Yet this judge is the very God in whom formerly even the spiritual had "hoped." At the revelation of the savior, however, Heracleon says that "all judgment has been given over to him." Now the demiurge, as judge, has come into the service of the higher powers. He becomes the savior's agent and avenger, who does the savior's will as his servant. The spiritual, then, who come to recognize their kinship with the higher powers, escape the judgment of the demiurge, having been united with those powers that transcend and direct his authority.

After citing the *apolytrōsis* formulae he attributes to the Marcosians, Irenaeus gives an account of their doctrines, returning in 1.13.21 to the subject of the *apolytrōsis*. Even here, he says, "there are as many schemes of *apolytrōsis* as there are mystagogues" (AH 1.21.1). He cites a number of these gnostic formulae that allegedly transcend the church's baptism, concluding with a liturgical dialogue formula that shows an affinity with the one cited in 1.13.5. Here the prayer is addressed not directly to the "Mother" but to the "powers" of the demiurge; yet the intention is similar. The initiate identifies himself as a "son of the pre-existent Father who has a pre-existent son." Claiming to have gnosis of "all things," and above all of Achamoth, the creative power above the demiurge, he concludes, "I derive being from him who is pre-existent, and I return to my own from which I came forth." In the second prayer, the initiate invokes the Mother, the "incorruptible Sophia," the pleromic Sophia, "who is in the Father." This formula, Irenaeus relates, is intended to confound the powers so that the initiate may pass beyond them into the *pleroma,* which is his own *topos.* "Having thrown off his bond, that is, his soul," he comes into "his own." [16]

Is it legitimate, however, to infer a more general circulation for these formulae than the Marcosian circle (to which Leisegang, for example, ascribes them [17]) ? To answer this question, one may first point out that Irenaeus himself announces that he is giving the views of various groups of gnostics (1.13.21). Epiphanius, in fact, ascribes these latter formulae not to the Marcosians, but specifically to the "followers of Heracleon" (Pan 36.2-6). This divergence of ascription suggests that the formulae represent a liturgical tradition common to several gnostic groups—a view which receives striking confirmation in the recently published First Apocalypse of James, from Nag Hammadi codex 5. There these same formulae recur almost *verbatim.* Böhlig and Labib, who have edited the manuscript, discount the possibility that Irenaeus used the Apocalypse as his source, and see evidence here for a common gnostic cult tradition. [18] In the Apocalypse the formulae are represented as part of a revelation the resurrected Lord gives to James, to enable James to disarm the "powers" which are "sons of the demiurge" and escape their jurisdiction. He is to do this by identifying himself with the Mother, Achamoth, and through her with the pre-existent Father himself. There the Lord promises that James "and all the sons of being" through the efficacy of these prayers, will pass through the regions of the demiurge's power, be saved and known by Sophia, and hidden in her.

---

[16] AH 1.21.5: »ἐγὼ υἱὸς ἀπὸ Πατρός, Πατρὸς προόντος, υἱὸς δὲ ἐν τῷ παρόντι· ἦλθον ⟨δὲ⟩ πάντα ἰδεῖν τὰ ἴδια καὶ τὰ ἀλλότρια, καὶ οὐκ ἀλλότρια δὲ παντελῶς, ἀλλὰ τῆς Ἀχαμώθ, ἥτις ἐστὶν θήλεια καὶ ταῦτα ἑαυτῇ ἐποίησεν. κατάγω δὲ τὸ γένος ἐκ τοῦ προόντος καὶ πορεύομαι πάλιν εἰς τὰ ἴδια, ὅθεν ἐλήλυθα«.

[17] H. Leisegang, *Die Gnosis* (Stuttgart, 1955, 4th ed.) , 348 f.

[18] 1 Apoc Jas 33.27 f; see the comments of Böhlig and Labib on pp. 32 and 43 f.

The other *apolytrōsis* formulae that Irenaeus cites stress less the negative function of distinguishing the "seed" so that they, by becoming identified with the higher powers, may escape the judgment, than the positive function of reuniting the "seed" that has been scattered and divided in the cosmos. As Theodotus says, although the male seed (the divine element) exists in unity, "we" (i.e., the "seed" in the cosmos) exist in separation. "For this reason," he says, "Jesus was baptized, to divide the undivided, until we should enter with them into the pleroma; that we, the many, becoming one, may be mingled in the one nature which was divided for our sake." [19] So, he says elsewhere, the "angels" (that is, the syzygies) are "baptized for us," and "we are baptized" to be "raised up" and "restored" into unity with them (Exc 22.1.7). Those baptized then "have the name," which signifies their union with their angelic syzygies. So the initiate, in one of the formulae Irenaeus cites, states that he "does not divide the spirit of Christ," and, in another, prays to enter "into the unity and redemption" of the Father (AH 1.21.3). This recalls the passage in Heracleon's exegesis of John, where the savior enjoins the woman (the female element of the seed) to be "redeemed" or "recovered" in order to be joined "in power and unity and mingling" with her syzygos (CJ 13.11).

To summarize, the Valentinians consider that the baptism of "the many" consists of a somatic aspect that washes the body, and a psychic aspect that releases the psychic from the prospect of death by conveying "forgiveness of sins." The spiritual baptism of the elect, which is *apolytrōsis,* on the other hand, releases the recipient from the psychic components of his cosmic existence, redeeming him altogether from the jurisdiction of the demiurge, and restoring him into unity with his pleroma, that is, with the "Mother" and "Father" beyond. Heracleon goes on to show that the "psychic" Christians interpret not only baptism but also the eucharist on the same somatic and psychic levels. He also indicates (as we shall see in the following chapter) how those who are pneumatic practice the eucharist "spiritually."

Heracleon intends, then, through his exegesis of the baptist, to characterize three modes of apprehending Christ. The level of sound is purely sensual. Voice is that which conveys meaning through sense-

[19] Exc 36.1-2: 1. Ἐν ἑνότητι μέντοι γε προεβλήθησαν οἱ ἄγγελοι ἡμῶν, φασίν, εἰσιόντες. ὡς ἀπὸ ἑνός προελθόντες. 2. ἐπεὶ δὲ ἡμεῖς ἦμεν, οἱ μεμερισμένοι, διὰ τοῦτο ἐβαπτίσατο ὁ Ἰησοῦς, τὸ ἀμέριστον μερισθῆναι, μέχρις ἡμᾶς ἐνώσῃ αὐτοῖς εἰς τὸ πλήρωμα, ἵνα ἡμεῖς, οἱ πολλοὶ ἓν γενόμενοι, [οἱ] πάντες τῷ ἑνὶ τῷ δι' ἡμᾶς μερισθέντι ἀνακραθῶμεν.

perceptible means. Logos, finally, is that level at which the sense-perceptible is itself perceived as symbolic of "spiritual realities" (CJ 13. 19). Those who stand at the first level consider Christ solely in terms of his outward appearance and circumstances. They consider him as the actual man Jesus who is the expected messiah of Israel. Those at the second level perceive him as the revelation of God, and yet can perceive him only as he is revealed in space and time. Those who are at the third level comprehend that the events described of Christ are actually themselves symbols of spiritual truth.

Analogously, to perceive baptism as a physical act is to remain at the hylic level of mere sense-perception. To interpret that act ethically as a sign of "forgiveness of sins" is to experience the transformation from "sound" into "voice," from the hylic to the psychic standpoint. This level of apprehension characterizes, according to Heracleon, the great majority of Christians. They remain at the psychic level, worshiping the psychic Christ as the son of the demiurge. These two levels of perception characterize the "baptism of John," that is, of the demiurge. Only those who transcend this—who receive from Christ himself the higher level of apprehension—receive the "pneumatic baptism" which is initiation into gnosis. Apparently Heracleon has in mind the sacrament of *apolytrōsis* as it was practiced in Valentinian communities.

Within Heracleon's exegesis, then, we can see how he has applied the metaphysical principle of the three ontological levels of being hermeneutically. The three "topoi" which John signifies topographically form the structure of all perception in general, as of exegesis in particular. The question that arises here—how men gain access to the different "topoi"—we defer until we have examined his exegesis of Christ's ascent to the higher topos.

4. The Temple (Jn 2) in Valentinian Exegesis

Heracleon and Origen agree that to practice "spiritual exegesis" is to interpret the places, objects, and events described in the text as symbols of spiritual reality. Origen accepts in practice the Valentinian analysis of three "levels" of exegesis—the literal (historical), ethical, and symbolic, or "spiritual." For this he alternatively has been praised as one of the developers of systematic exegesis and has been accused of "gnostic" and "spiritualizing" tendencies. He declares, for example, that the literal, apart from the "higher levels" of exegesis, is in itself meaningless in terms of the Christian's present experience.[1] Origen, however, insists that the "literal meaning" must be accepted and sus-

[1] CJ 10.43: "How can anyone be said to fully believe in the scripture (πιστεύειν . . . τῇ γραφῇ) when he does not see in it the mind of the holy spirit (τὸν ἐν αὐτῇ τοῦ ἁγίου πνεύματος νοῦν) which God would have us believe rather than the literal meaning (τοῦ γράμματους θέλημα)? We must say, therefore, that those who 'walk according to the flesh' [i.e., the literal] believe none of the spiritual things of the law; not even the first principle of these things is revealed to them." So also he explains in CJ 10.17, where he interprets the passover lamb as an allegory of scripture, that to read literally is to "eat the flesh of the lamb raw"; it is to be irrationally enslaved "to the letter." Pneumatic exegesis converts these "raw materials" into spiritually nourishing "food." His whole discussion from CJ 10.15-18 and 10.24-27 shows the impossibility of literal exegesis. He sets forth the principle of his own exegesis in distinction from literalism, on the one hand, and from traditional typological exegesis on the other: CJ 10.18: "One must not regard historical things as types of historical things, and material things as types of material, but the material are types of spiritual things, and the historical of the intelligible."

THE TEMPLE (JN 2) IN VALENTINIAN EXEGESIS

tained in this process—that it forms, in fact, the primary foundation for the higher levels of exegesis.[2] Heracleon, on the other hand, understands his exegesis as a method of systematically translating somatic "images" into spiritual truth (CJ 13.19). Unlike Origen, he regards the "literal" as relevant to exegesis only insofar as it is understood metaphorically. "In itself"—in its own terms—the literal remains for the pneumatic an obstacle, potentially a source of error and ignorance.

While Origen, then, at the first level of his exegesis, concerns himself with the actual geography of Palestine, Heracleon disdains geographical considerations altogether (CJ 6.40). With regard to Jn 2.12-21, Heracleon first explains what Jesus' "descent into Capernaum" signifies—the "beginning of a new oikonomia" (CJ 10.11). As we have seen, Heracleon describes this "region" wholly in metaphorical terms. He says that as Capernaum lies in the lower part of the intermediate topos, toward the lowest point, the sea, it symbolizes total immersion in matter (CJ 13.60). This represents the topos of the devil, or of his "cosmos," which consists of "the whole hylē, the totality of evil," or "the desert inhabited by wild beasts." [3] This region is alien to the savior and remains incapable of receiving him. It is the home of the devil's "own," the hylics. Their spiritual condition is therefore one of total ignorance (agnoia).

After his fruitless descent to Capernaum, the savior reascends "to Jerusalem" (Jn 2.13). The ascent also is interpreted symbolically. It signifies "the ascent from the hylic regions into the psychic region (topos)." Jerusalem, signifying the "psychic topos," is the "place" of the demiurge, whom "the Jews" worship. Heracleon notes that it is the earthly Jerusalem that symbolizes the psychic topos, and not the "Jerusalem above" (CJ 10.33).

To understand his characterization of this topos, we must consider how he regards "the Jews" who dwell there. Are we to assume that, when Heracleon considers "the Jews" in John, he understands by this the actual members of the twelve tribes, the nation of Israel? Three observations prevent us from taking his use of the term literally. First, as noted above, a literal interpretation of "the Jews" as the people of Israel would contradict his usual exegetical practice of interpreting

---

[2] For discussion, see Gögler, *Zur Theologie des biblischen Wortes bei Origenes* (Düsseldorf, 1963), 299-364. Origen consistently sustains the validity of the history, together with the actuality of the incarnation, as the basic presupposition for all exegesis: cf CJ 10.3-5.

[3] CJ 13.16: ὄρος μὲν τὸν διάβολον λέγεσθαι ἢ τὸν κόσμον αὐτοῦ, ἐπείπερ μέρος ἓν ὁ διάβολος ὅλης τῆς ὕλης, φησίν, ἦν, ὁ δὲ κόσμος τὸ σύμπαν τῆς κακίας ὄρος, ἔρημον οἰκητήριον θηρίων, ᾧ προσεκύνουν πάντες οἱ πρὸ νόμου καὶ οἱ ἐθνικοί·

literal phenomena as symbols of spiritual reality. Secondly, none of the fragments indicate that Heracleon shared with the mainstream of second-century Christians any concern over their relation to the Jewish community or the people of Israel. His concern instead is to define, among *Christians*, the relation between those who remain at the "psychic level" and those who attain to the "spiritual." Third, the "God of the Jews," in his terminology, designates not simply the God of Jewish religion, but the creator whom "psychic Christians" also worship as their God.

When Heracleon explains, then, that Jerusalem, the "psychic topos," is that of "the Jews," he goes on to explain that the levites, the sanctified tribe of "Jews" who serve in the temple courtyard, are "a symbol of those psychics who attain salvation" (CJ 10.33). In other words, these are no more "Jews" for him in a literal sense than John the baptist is an actual person. Heracleon consistently interprets "the Jews" in John as the representation of the *psychics*. The "levites" among them are those psychics who are converted to believe in the savior.

Conversely, he interprets the gentiles, and in this case especially the Samaritan woman of Jn 4, as a symbol for the "pneumatics." She becomes the symbol of the pneumatic, while "Abraham's son," a "Jew," represents the psychic who is converted and saved (see below, pp. 83 f).

This same interpretation of the terms recurs in the Valentinian exegesis of Rom 3 and 4 preserved in fragments of Origen's commentary on Romans. Here again, the Valentinian exegete (whether Heracleon or not, we do not know) designates "the circumcised," the "Jews," who are "Abraham's children according to the flesh," as "psychics." The "race of Ishmael," that is, the gentiles, who are "Jews in secret" (cf Rom 3.29-30) represents the pneumatics.[4] A preliminary investigation into other gnostic texts[5] suggests that this interpretation may represent a widespread and technical use of these terms.

The temple as an image of the ecclesia

According to Heracleon, when the savior ascends to this psychic topos (Jerusalem) and goes into the sanctuary (*naos*), he first enters

[4] CR 5.3 f Scherer, *Commentaire*, 143 f, and especially 15 (168-169). Puech and Quispel ("Quatrième Ecrit" 73) also have noted how the terms "Jew" and "Gentile" are used technically in Valentinian exegesis to designate psychics and pneumatics respectively.
[5] Cf Gospel of Philip 1.4.6.

the temple courtyard, the "place" of the "levites." This demonstrates that the savior comes to help the "many" who are "called" (a technical term for psychics) as well as the "few" (that is, the pneumatics) who are "the chosen" (CJ 10.33; 13.31; 13.51: see Mt 22.14). The "holy of holies," where the savior finally enters is the highest "place" of all, the topos reserved for pneumatics. The inner temple, then, symbolically interpreted, represents the "pneumatic ecclesia."

By Heracleon's time, such interpretation of the temple already has received a long tradition. The gospel of John, for example, "attempts to give clear expression to the idea that Jesus himself is the 'new' temple of the messianic age." [6] Jesus himself has become the locus of God's presence among men. "The new fellowship in replacement of the temple . . . is created through that Jesus whose body has passed through the gates of death and resurrection." [7] The author of John places the account of Jesus' cleansing the temple (Jn 2.13-17) directly before the saying "destroy this temple, and in three days I will raise it up" (Jn 2.19). The epistles, on the other hand, present a different view:

The epistles never say that Jesus is the "new" temple; it is always the community, the Church, which has this position. It is true that this "new" temple is brought into being through Christ or the Spirit, but the actual temple is the collective, the community, as in Qûmran. [8]

In the deutero-Pauline corpus, the believers are described as being "built up" into a "holy temple" on the "foundation of the apostles and the prophets," with Jesus Christ as the "cornerstone" (Eph 2.19-22), a parallel to the "living stones" of 1 Pet 2.5. In Eph 4.11-16, the author uses Paul's description of the church as Christ's body (1 Cor 12.27 f) as an alternative description of the church.

Schlier has suggested that the conception of the "body of Christ" in Ephesians derives neither from Paul nor from a development of Pauline theology, but from the influence of the gnostic redeemer myth. From an examination of parallel sources such as the Acts of Philip 144, the Manichean writings, and the Naassene preaching, Schlier suggests that the consummation of the "body of Christ" in Ephesians is parallel to the consummation of the gnostic "divine Anthropos" as the head of his own pleroma. In both conceptions, the totality of the

[6] B. Gärtner, *The Temple and the Community in Qûmran and in the New Testament* (SNTS Monograph 1, Cambridge, 1965), 119.

[7] Gärtner, *Temple*, 120.

[8] Gärtner, *Temple*, 121.

"seed" sown into the world is to be regathered to reconstitute the original pleromic Anthropos.[9]

Ernst Käsemann, following Schlier, has attempted to clarify the concept of the body of Christ by comparison with the Naassene preaching, the Acts of Thomas (ch. 6) and the Excerpts from Theodotus (33.2), where Christ is called the "head" of the "seed" who are to enter into the pleroma. Käsemann points out that the Anthropos of the Naassene preaching is also called the "cornerstone," set "into the foundations of Zion." The construction stones are "alive" (empsychoi) and "grow"—they are the "spiritual." The "heavenly dwelling" into which they are being built is the archetype of their earthly dwelling. The anthropological theory underlying this image is that of the true "inner man" who dwells in the body as in a residence. In bodily existence he is confined and oppressed by his material body and by the "powers" that rule over it. From this oppression those who share in the archetype of Adam are to be regathered into him, reconstituting the original anthropos—he is their heavenly "home" (oikos).[10]

Anti-gnostic Christians also develop comprehensive theological interpretations of the temple. This development can be traced prior to Origen's time through such writers as Ignatius, Hermas, Barnabas, Polycarp, Irenaeus, and Clement of Alexandria. This tradition includes reference of the temple symbolism to Jesus himself, to his own body, as well as to "his body" the church (in both the individual and collective sense).[11]

Heracleon's designation of the Jerusalem temple as an image of the spiritual church flows, then, from a varied tradition. If, as he interprets Jn 2, he has in mind the reunion of the pleromic aions Anthropos and Ecclesia, he is consistent in his practice of omitting direct mention of the pleromic myth. More clearly demonstrable is Valentinus' influence. In a fragment of his ethical teaching preserved by Clement of Alexandria, Valentinus describes the human "heart" as an inn indwelt and overrun by evil spirits: "in this way the heart, unless some providence intervenes, is impure, being the dwelling place of many demons." But, he continues, "when the good Father looks upon it, it is sanctified and illuminated with light, and the one who has such a heart is blessed" (Strom 2.[20.]114). The process of purification,

---

[9] H. Schlier, Christus und die Kirche im Epheserbrief (Mohr, 1930), 37-48.

[10] E. Käsemann, Leib und Leib Christi (Tübingen, 1933); P. Vielhauer, Oikodome (Karlsruhe, 1940), 34-55; H. Jonas, Gnosis und spätantiker Geist (Göttingen, 1954), 100-102.

[11] For summary and citations, see Vielhauer, Oikodome, 154-172.

which both Heracleon and Valentinus describe, apparently applies equally to the whole spiritual ecclesia as to its individual members.

Heracleon's ecclesiology is most clearly traceable to the allegory of the temple in Heb 9. He refers directly to this passage (which he almost certainly considers Pauline) and follows its structure in his own ecclesiological description. Heb 9 relates that the "first" covenant has prescribed commandments for worship in a cosmic sanctuary (*hagion kosmikon,* 9.1). The forecourt of this temple is accessible to the "priests" (9.6) who offer there gifts and sacrifices that fail to "perfect" them (9.10). Behind the "second veil" (9.3) stands the "holy of holies"; into this inner sanctuary "only the high priest enters" (9.7). There Christ through the spirit offers himself as high priest to the "living God" (9.14). The worship he offers occurs in the "true" and "heavenly" temple, of which the first is only an "antitype" (9.23), a "parable of the present age" (9.9).

Heracleon, who takes the "Jews" of Hebrews as an image of the "psychic Christians," claims that these Christians fail to distinguish between the "cosmic" antitypes and the pneumatic realities symbolized thereby (CJ 13.19). The temple forecourt for him symbolizes the "psychic topos" accessible to the "levites"—to the "psychics who are saved." But their topos remains "cosmic"; it fails to offer a means of "perfecting" them. The "holy of holies" where "only the high priest may enter" symbolizes the pneumatic topos accessible to the pneumatics through the savior (CJ 10.33). There they worship "in spirit and truth" not the demiurge but the "living God" (cf Heb 9.14) who is "the father" (CJ 13.19; cf Jn 4.24). Their pneumatic worship is "rational worship" (CJ 13.25; cf Rom 12.1). And as the author of Hebrews contrasts Christ's first appearance to "bear the sins of many" with his second appearance to receive "those expecting him" (9.28), so Heracleon contrasts the "many psychics" (CJ 13.51) who need forgiveness of sins with the "single-formed" pneumatic ecclesia that "expects" his coming (CJ 13.51; 13.27-28).

Exc 27.1 f offers another Valentinian exegesis of the ecclesiology of Hebrews. But here the exegete describes the entrance into the "holy of holies" not as the present prerogative of the pneumatics but as the future prospect of the psychics themselves. As in Heracleon's exegesis, the "priestly service" belongs to the *oikonomia* (Exc 27.6; cf Heb 9.9). The passage describes how the "priest," having been purified through his previous service in the forecourt, finally puts off the psychic component of his existence, the "body of the soul" (Exc 27.1). Leaving

71

the "cosmic" behind, he passes into the "noetic cosmos," into the holy of holies "behind the second veil." He transcends the sphere of the "principalities and powers" (Exc 27.2) and the "angelic teaching" (Exc 27.3) so that becoming "truly rational and high priestly" he receives life from the logos, becomes a logos (Exc 27.5), and sees God "face to face" (cf 1 Cor 12.12).

Does this exegesis contradict Heracleon's? I suggest that it does not, although its focus differs. The author of Exc 27 interprets the temple allegory in terms of the consummation, while Heracleon interprets it in terms of the present *oikonomia*. Apparently the author of Exc 27 agrees with Heracleon that during the *oikonomia* the psychic "priests" continue to offer only "priestly service" (27.6). Heracleon agrees with him, in turn, that the psychics themselves may finally receive the logos and the "truth itself" (CJ 13.44; 13.53) which pneumatics receive in the present. Heracleon indicates that those who are presently psychic are to gain access into the pleromic "holy of holies" where pneumatics are worshiping already (CJ 10.33; 13.44). But in CJ 10.33, Heracleon intends to describe the situation of the present age, in which psychic believers and the pneumatic elect stand at distinctly different *topoi* in relation to God: the psychics remain in the forecourt "outside," while the pneumatics alone dwell within the "holy of holies."

For Heracleon (as for Valentinus) the Johannine account of the cleansing of the inner temple becomes an allegory for the purification of the "spiritual ecclesia"—of the pneumatics themselves. To recognize this is crucial for our understanding of his soteriology, for it contradicts the usual simplistic understanding of the Valentinian doctrine of the "spiritual." What "purification" would they need, if they are (as so many commentators have repeated from Clement) "saved by nature," or, for that matter, if they are (as we claim) not "substantially determined" but elected to salvation?

Heracleon (like Valentinus), nevertheless, clearly indicates that the "spiritual" who are the "chosen," need the savior to minister to them and to purify them. He explains that their fault is not "sins," but that of misapprehending the basis of their relation to God. The savior, entering into their topos, finds some among them who are "merchandizing and money-changing." Heracleon explains that these are those who regard their own task of evangelizing as a means of accumulating spiritual "gain and profit." They administer worship and welcome newcomers as if for their own advantage. Such members of the elect are guilty of "attributing nothing to grace." [12] Priding themselves on their spiritual position, they attempt to gain advantage from it. In this they fail above all to recognize the gratuity of the grace they have received. Although they are the "house of God," that is, Heracleon explains, of the Father of Christ, they (as Valentinus had described) have been invaded by alien powers.

According to the account, Jesus takes a scourge he makes out of cords and purges the "evil powers" from their midst. This description of events must be symbolically understood. The scourge, the cords, and the garment Jesus wears, Heracleon explains, are "images of the power and energy of the holy spirit." The cords could not have been made "from the skin of a dead animal, but from woven reeds"; and being fashioned from wood, the scourge offers a "type of the cross." By this "wood," by the cross, "the speculators, the merchants, and all evil have been nailed up and annihilated." Through this instrument, the symbol of the powers of spirit and the cross, the savior purifies and reconstitutes the ecclesia, so that, no longer invaded by thieves and merchants, it becomes truly the "house of his Father." The alien powers which had defiled the ecclesia are cast out and destroyed. As they flee from the savior, they cry out in the words of the psalm, "the zeal for your house has devoured me" (CJ 10.33).

The sign of the cross, which appears in the scourge, raises the question of how Heracleon interprets the passion of Chirst. He has said already that the passion is a "sign" (sēmeion) —a view which recurs in his interpretation of the scourge. Origen relates that Heracleon interprets all the events of Christ's coming, his life, and death, as "images of the things that are in the pleroma" (CJ 13.19). A parallel passage from the Excerpts from Theodotus suggests more precisely what the "sign" of the cross may mean for Heracleon. According to Exc 42.1f,

the cross is a sign (sēmeion) of the limit (horou) in the pleroma, for it divides the unfaithful from the faithful as that divides the cosmos from the pleroma. Therefore Jesus by that sign carries the seed on his shoulders and leads them into the pleroma. For Jesus is called the shoulders and Christ is the head. . . . Therefore he took the body of Jesus which is of the same being (homoousios) as the ecclesia.

In Exc 22.4, similarly, the cross is associated with the power of horos (limit). It hinders some from entering into the pleroma, and

[12] CJ 10.33: ἀντὶ τῶν μηδὲν χάριτι διδόντων, ἀλλ' ἐμπορίαν καὶ κέρδος τὴν τῶν ξένων εἰς τὸ ἱερὸν εἴσοδον νομιζόντων, τοῦ ἰδίου κέρδους καὶ φιλαργυρίας ἕνεκεν τὰς εἰς τὴν λατρείαν τοῦ θεοῦ θυσίας χορηγούντων.

it delivers others to enter into the pleroma by dividing them from the cosmos. Irenaeus also states that the separating and dividing function is called *horos,* and the supporting and sustaining function is called *stauros* (cross). Irenaeus mentions a Valentinian exegesis of Lk 3.17, which says that "the fan is in his hand, to clear his threshing floor, and to gather the wheat into his granary, but the chaff he will burn with unquenchable fire." Irenaeus adds that "the fan they explain to be the cross *(stauros)* which consumes . . . all materiality, as fire does chaff, but it purifies all those who are saved, as a fan does wheat" (AH 1.3.4-5). As *horos* separated and delivered the exiled Sophia from her passion, so the savior has come into the cosmos "for the passion" to deliver "us," that is, the spiritual, "from passions." Irenaeus relates that the savior's passion on the cross is interpreted as a "sign" of the redemption:

They say that the Lord has come in the last times of the cosmos for this, for the passion, in order to manifest the passion that occurred to the last of the aions, and through his own end, he might manifest the end of the matter concerning the aions (AH 1.8.1-2).[18]

The savior on the cross, then, set forth through his own passion a "sign" of the passion of Sophia, the archetype of the spiritual ecclesia. In manifesting her suffering and her redemption, the savior manifests to the elect their own, as it occurs through the process of purification *(horos)* and sustenance *(stauros)* which the cross symbolizes.

The Gospel of Truth offers another way, related to this, of elucidating the symbolism of the cross. In 20.25 f, the author says that the "names of the elect" are revealed when Christ "fastens the declaration of the Father's will" to the cross. When their election is thus revealed, the spiritual may ascend to the Father. They may, in the words of Exc 76.1, "follow him" into the pleroma.

Heracleon also shows how the cross serves to purify the elect, annihilating every false claim to spiritual priority, apart from the "grace" to which alone they owe their election. In this way also, he shows how the cross as well as the temple are to be interpreted by the spiritual as "signs" and symbols of spiritual truth.

Yet the temple, which spiritually interpreted symbolizes the pneumatic ecclesia, may also receive psychic and hylic interpretations. On a

[18] AH 1.8.1-2: τὸν κύριον ἐν τοῖς ἐσχάτοις τοῦ κόσμου χρόνοις διὰ τοῦτο ἐληλυθέναι ἐπὶ τὸ πάθος λέγουσιν, ἵν᾽ ἐπιδείξῃ τὸ περὶ τὸν ἔσχατον τῶν Αἰώνων γεγονὸς πάθος καὶ διὰ τούτου τοῦ τέλους ἐμφήνῃ τὸ τέλος τῆς περὶ τοὺς Αἰῶνας πραγματείας.

psychic level, it represents the physical body of Jesus; on a hylic level, the ancient temple of Solomon prefigures it as a material type (CJ 10.38). So also the other terms may be interpreted on each of the three levels. The passover, considered from the "standpoint" of the hylic topos, is the ancient festival of Israel. On a psychic level, that festival is seen as a prefiguration of the passion and death of Jesus (CJ 10.19). Heracleon indicates that he is well aware that this "psychic" interpretation of the passover prevails among many Christians. Such a typological and historical interpretation of passover occurs in the writings of such authors as Justin, Irenaeus, Melito, and Hippolytus. Hippolytus, for example, regards the preparation of the passover lamb as a detailed prophecy of the events of Christ's passion. The passover, seen as prophetic, is "fulfilled" typologically in Jesus' death (Comm Matt 10). Within the emerging mainstream of Christian traditions, from the writings of Paul through those of the above-named authors, such typological exegesis of the passover becomes the theological basis for the most widely used forms of eucharistic theology.[14]

Heracleon's criticism of non-Valentinian eucharistic theology

Heracleon, however, regards this typological interpretation in which Jesus' death is the fulfillment of the passover "type" as an interpretation which remains merely "psychic." The eucharistic theology which follows from it remains (in his view) like the corresponding interpretation of baptism—on the somatic and psychic levels alone. For it is characteristic of psychics, he says, that they mistake the images of spiritual reality for the reality itself. Just as they worship the one they call "creator," who is himself only a "creation," an image of the Father above, so also they center their faith on the actual physical Jesus, and on the somatic events of his life and death, which they interpret psychically. Nowhere is this clearer than in their celebration of the eucharist. For they interpret the sacrament in terms of the "passion of the savior in the cosmos." They refer first to the "lamb," which, as Heracleon has explained, means Jesus' physical body (CJ 6.60). Then they interpret the somatic event of the "slaying of the lamb," that is, the death of Jesus, in psychic terms, as a "sacrifice" offered for "forgiveness of sins" (Mt 26.28). As the baptist proclaims

---

[14] For a summary, see J. Daniélou, *From Shadows to Reality* (transl. by W. Hibberd of *Sacramentum Futuri: Etudes sur les Origines de la Typologie biblique;* London, 1960), 115-130.

in his psychic role as "voice," that "sacrifice" of the lamb, the death of Jesus, "takes away the sins of the world" (Jn 1.29). They interpret the eucharistic "eating" as the "recalling" (*anamnēsis*) of the Lord's death and parousia (1 Cor 11.23-26). Centering their eucharistic theology and practice on the "images" they mistake for reality, they worship "in flesh and error."

Thus in the typology of the early "mainstream" authors, the "type" of the passover is said to receive its "fulfillment" and "reality" in the death of Jesus. Heracleon does not deny that this interpretation of the eucharist may bear a certain validity—at least on the psychic level. But those who are spiritual will recognize that such psychic interpretation falls into the same error as the Jews—the error of mistaking the "type" for the "reality" (CJ 13.19). The spiritual perceive that the event of Jesus' death is not so much the "reality" of an OT "type," but is itself a "type" (CJ 10.19) given in concrete and historical terms to symbolize a spiritual reality. Interpreting the passion and death of Jesus as themselves "types" opens up the possibility of seeing in them higher and more symbolic meaning than the psychics perceive. While the psychics actually worship as "Jews," celebrating the eucharist, in terms of historical typology, as the "passover of the Jews," the spiritual perceive the realities of which the passion and death of Christ are types, and thereby celebrate it instead as the "divine passover" (cf CJ 10.13).

Heracleon indicates how each of the terms of the psychic eucharistic interpretation may bear a higher, symbolic meaning. For the *passion,* he says, may recall not only the *slain lamb* (i.e., the historical death of Jesus) "but also the eternal life there offered." The *sacrifice* means not only, as for psychics, forgiveness of sins, but also, for the spiritual, "what the passion of the savior signified in the cosmos." The *eating* of it anticipates not only the Lord's parousia, as for psychics, but also the savior's marriage feast in the eschatological "marriage" with the elect.

Of what, then, is the passion a "type," if not of the death of Jesus which offers forgiveness of sins? What does it "symbolize"? Irenaeus' account gives the answer which seems to represent generally accepted Valentinian tradition: "They say that the Lord has come in the last times of the cosmos for this purpose—for the passion, in order to manifest the passion of the last of the aions. Through his own end he intends to show the end of the matter concerning the aions" (AH 1.8.1-2). The sufferings of the savior have symbolized what she (Sophia) suffered. The anguish, sense of abandonment, fear, and resourceless-ness he experiences symbolize hers, as his cross is a sign of her restora-tion.

Theodotus gives a somewhat revised version of this tradition. He says that in the savior's passion not only the "whole pleroma" but *also* the "seed" participated. The "whole" (i.e., the pleroma) and the "all" (the seed) both experienced there the "loss of the name." In the restoration of Sophia, the "seed," as well as the "whole pleroma," re-cover the name, receiving the gnosis of the Father.[15]

Comparison with the version Irenaeus gives, on the one hand, and that of Heracleon and the Gospel of Truth on the other, suggests that Theodotus here intends to show how the passion of Sophia in the pre-cosmic drama—which alone is mentioned in Irenaeus' account—applies to the existential situation of the "seed," i.e., the elect in the cosmos. This apparently involves a revision of Valentinian myth to place it in existential terms. If this is indeed what Theodotus intends, Heracleon and the author of the Gospel of Truth complete this process of demythologizing. That they describe the process of redemption in a way structurally analogous to the process described in the myth indicates that they, as Valentinian theologians, presuppose its validity. But they interpret the savior's passion *without* direct reference to the myth, describing the process of redemption not in terms of Sophia's fall and restoration, but in terms of the "existential" situation of the "seed," the elect in the cosmos.

The author of the Gospel of Truth, as noted above, intends to show how, at Christ's death, the "all," that is, the "totality" of the seed, which has been lost and alienated, becomes manifest as the elect of the Father. Through the cross the "Testament" of the Father, previously hidden, is manifested, revealing the *names* of those "whom the Father foreknew" (Ev Ver 11.21) . As in the Theodotus' account, they recover the name and the gnosis of their spiritual identity in him.

For Heracleon also, the "passion of the savior" signifies "pleromic realities"—the term apparently an oblique reference to the pre-cosmic passion of Sophia. Strikingly, however, he never mentions Sophia directly, even in his exegesis of the Samaritan woman at the well—whose experience so closely parallels that of Sophia that Sagnard says

---

[15] Exc 31.1: Ἀλλὰ καὶ εἰ ὁ κατελθὼν εὐδοκία τοῦ ὅλου ἦν (»ἐν αὐτῷ γὰρ πᾶν τὸ πλήρωμα ἦν σωματικῶς«) , ἔπαθεν δὲ οὗτος, δῆλον ὅτι καὶ τὰ ἐν αὐτῷ σπέρματα συνέπαθεν, δι' ὧν τὸ ὅλον καὶ τὸ πᾶν εὑρίσκεται πάσχον.

she must symbolize Sophia.[16] Heracleon, however, consistently calls her the "pneumatic ecclesia"—that is, the divine "seed" as it is manifest in the cosmos—not Sophia, but her *cosmic* counterpart (CJ 13.27). What the *passion of the savior* symbolizes, then, is the process of recovering and restoring the lost "seed" into unity and gnosis of the Father. Heracleon's basic premise for interpreting the savior's passion, then, accords with that found in the other accounts. The passion of the savior must not be interpreted "somatically," in terms of the death of Jesus, nor only "psychically," in terms of the forgiveness of sins: "spiritually" it refers on a higher level to the passion of the divine ecclesia and to her restoration to her spiritual identity.

The church's eucharistic theory and practice (which the Valentinians describe as "psychic") is relatively well known from second-century sources. Its theology centers, as Heracleon says, on the *anamnēsis* of the death of Jesus, which is interpreted primarily as a sacrifice made for the forgiveness of sins (cf Mt 26.28). It also "proclaims that death" (1 Cor 11.26) in anticipation of the Lord's parousia. Of Valentinian eucharistic theology and practice, on the other hand, we know little beyond the hints Heracleon offers. Here again, we may examine the formulae Irenaeus attributes to the Marcosians. If the eucharistic formulae, like the *apolytrōsis* formulae, also represent a common gnostic cult tradition, they may offer an analogy to Heracleon's statements.

The Valentinian sacrament of the "bridechamber"

Irenaeus describes how the gnostics around Marcus, "pretending to practice the eucharist" (*eucharistein*) have extended the invocation (*epiklēsis*) formula which they pronounce over a cup of mixed wine. The utterance of this formula is regarded as an act of sacramental transformation, so that the wine becomes the blood—not of Jesus, but of Charis, "one of those (aions) beyond all things." Uttering the epiklesis formula, the celebrant then offers the cup to the congregation to drink, "in order that the grace (*charis*) may flow into them" (AH 1.13.2 f).

For the ritual acts Irenaeus describes, Heracleon's extant fragments offer no counterpart. For the phrases of the epiklesis prayer, however, Heracleon does give some striking analogies. The first prayer reads,

[16] *Gnose,* 502: "One sees, incidentally, that the Samaritan is the 'Sophia' of Irenaeus' account (as also of Theodotus'). This cannot be doubted: all the characteristics correspond exactly."

May the unimaginable and ineffable Charis, who is before all things, fill you in your inner man (*anthrōpon*) and multiply in you the *gnosis* of her, sowing the mustard seed in you as in good ground.[17]

Such a prayer corresponds to Heracleon's description of the elect, who are not to consider their election in terms of their own spiritual advantage or gain, thereby "attributing nothing to grace" (CJ 10.33). For unlike those whose salvation depends upon their own works, the elect receive "imperishable grace" as "wealth furnished from above" (CJ 13.10). Yet whoever receives this grace, receives it not in his natural existence, but in his "inner man," which is the "life" formed in him by the logos (CJ 2.21). The recognition of one's own election is *gnosis,* or, as in this formula, the "gnosis of grace (*charis*)." The statement that grace has prepared the elect by "sowing them as seed in good ground" correlates with Heracleon's exegesis of the harvest parable in Jn 4. There he describes how the elect are "sown from above" as "seed" into cosmic creation (CJ 13.49). The angels of the oikonomia serve as the means of this sowing, themselves "cultivating the ground," which is apparently the material counterpart of the "seed" (CJ 13.50). Heracleon describes not only the "sowing," but also how the seed grows and "ripens" at different rates, until all those sown are "ripe and ready" for the savior to send his angels (the syzygies) as "reapers for the harvest."

Accordingly, then, Heracleon might see such an epiklesis prayer as intended to remind the elect that they owe their election to "the grace of the powers beyond the cosmos," and to pray that the seed may grow toward maturity (*teliōsis*) as he himself describes that process, being sown into the "good ground" of the community gathered for the sacrament.

Heracleon has also said that the "eating" anticipates, for the spiritual, the "rest in the marriage." This suggests, according to the analogy above, that, if the first prayer, referring to the pre-cosmic sowing, pleads for the fulfillment of the present process of growth toward maturity, the second anticipates the future consummation. The second prayer reads,

I will for you to share in my grace, since the Father of all beholds your angel in his presence. The place (topos) of the greatness in us is through us to be established. Take first this grace from me and through me. Prepare yourself

[17] AH 1.13.2: »ἡ πρὸ τῶν ὅλων, ἡ ἀνεννόητος καὶ ἄρρητος Χάρις πληρῶσαί σου τὸν ἔσω ἄνθρωπον καὶ πληθῦναι ἐν σοὶ τὴν γνῶσιν αὐτῆς, ἐγκατασπείρουσα τὸν κόκκον τοῦ σινάπεως εἰς τὴν ἀγαθὴν γῆν«.

as a bride receiving her bridegroom, that you may be what I am, and I what you are. Consecrate in your bridechamber the seed of light. Take from me the bridegroom, and receive him, and be received by him. Behold, grace has come upon you. Open your mouth, and prophesy.[18]

Comparison with Heracleon's statements suggests that the celebrant speaks here as the savior. For, according to Heracleon, it is the savior who gives the bridegroom to the bride. The "bride," Heracleon tells us, is the elect on earth, who are (as Clement also relates) the "female element" of the seed (Exc 21.1-22). The one addressed must be, then, the elect, enjoined in the sacrament to prepare "to receive the bride-groom." The basis for this command is her election—that the Father (whose will is expressed through the savior; CJ 13.38; Ev Ver 11.23 f), *wills* for her to share in "his grace." Being elect, the recipient has an "angel," that is, the spiritual identity which Heracleon calls her "hus-band in the pleroma," here called her "angel" whom the Father beholds "in his presence." As, in Heracleon's account, the savior commands the elect on earth to "call her husband," so here the elect are enjoined to "prepare to receive" the divine bridegroom. Heracleon says the elect are called "to be married to him by the savior, in power and unity and conjunction" in a marriage the Valentinians saw figured in the marriage at Cana (CJ 13.11). There, as the savior transformed water into wine, so the human is to be transformed into the divine. The transformation ritual that Irenaeus contemptuously dismisses as a magic trick (that the celebrant makes the liquid in the cup appear to be red and purple) may have been intended as a symbol for that process of transformation.

The participants are to become "what he (the savior) is": so He-racleon also has explained that the angelic syzygies are "of the same divine nature" as the logos and savior (CJ 13.25). Their human counterparts must become transformed into the divine. This, ap-parently, is the "consecration of the seed of light." From the savior the elect sacramentally receives the syzygos, here in anticipation of the great "marriage" in which the "whole seed," reunited with its divine counterpart, will enter finally into the "ineffable marriage of syzygies," in the true "bridechamber" that is the pleroma (AH 1.7.1).

---

[18] AH 1.13.3: »μεταδοῦναί σοι θέλω τῆς ἐμῆς Χάριτος, ἐπειδὴ ὁ πατὴρ τῶν ὅλων τὸν ἄγγελόν σου διὰ παντὸς βλέπει πρὸ προσώπου αὐτοῦ. ὁ δὲ τόπος τοῦ Μεγέθους ἐν ἡμῖν ἐστι· δεῖ ἡμᾶς εἰς τὸ ἓν καταστῆναι. λάμβανε πρῶτον ἀπ' ἐμοῦ καὶ δι' ἐμοῦ τὴν Χάριν. εὐτρέπισον σεαυτὴν ὡς νύμφη ἐκδεχομένη τὸν νυμφίον ἑαυτῆς, ἵνα ἔσῃ ὃ ἐγὼ καὶ ἐγὼ ὃ σύ. καθίδρυσον ἐν τῷ νυμφῶνί σου τὸ σπέρμα τοῦ φωτός. λάβε παρ' ἐμοῦ τὸν νυμφίον καὶ χώρησον αὐτὸν καὶ χωρήθητι ἐν αὐτῷ. ἰδού, ἡ Χάρις κατῆλθεν ἐπὶ σέ· ἄνοιξον τὸ στόμα σου καὶ προφήτευσον«.

The last injunction of the prayer—the command to prophesy—has no counterpart in the Heracleon fragments. The evidence from Heracleon is too sparse to follow out a correlation with the liturgical evidence in every detail; the correspondence we find, although striking, remains incomplete. If Irenaeus knows these prayers, as he says, from a Marcosian liturgy, our analysis suggests that these eucharistic formulae, like the *apolytrōsis* formulae, were disseminated beyond the Marcosian circle, or, conversely, were borrowed by the Marcosians from more widely known Valentinian liturgy. Should they recur, as have the *apolytrōsis* formulae, in newly available manuscripts, one would have independent evidence for their more general use.

Our analysis of Heracleon's fragments, then, indicates that the Valentinians clearly differentiated between the sacramental practice and doctrine of the "great church" and that of the gnostic initiates. In their view the "psychic church," offers only the "baptism of John" (that is, of the demiurge) in two aspects: they perform the somatic act of washing with water, and they may receive the psychic benefit of "forgiveness of sins" that grants them a "capacity for salvation" if they persist in good works. The "spiritual ecclesia" consisting of the elect alone, receives the third and higher baptism, the "redemption of Christ," which redeems the elect from the psychic elements of their own existence and from the power of the demiurge. It conveys the spirit which brings them "to perfection," and restores them to unity with the pleroma. The psychics also celebrate a eucharist which "somatically" commemorates the historical death of Jesus, which they interpret "psychically" as a "sacrifice for sins." What they celebrate, however, "in flesh and error," is actually (from the Valentinian point of view) the "passover of the Jews," since they mistake the historical events, themselves "types," for reality. The spiritual, however, comprehend the "passion of the savior" as the symbol of their own restoration to the father. They alone celebrate the "divine passover" that recalls to them the grace of their election, invokes the grace that brings them to maturity in the present, and anticipates the eschatological "marriage" in which they are to become one "in spirit" with the Father.

Valentinian teaching on the pneumatic ecclesia always contains—whether stated or not—an implicit comparison with those who are only psychic. As we have seen, Heracleon does not deny to psychics the possibility of attaining "salvation." Even those who are saved, however, insofar as they *remain* psychic, remain outside the pleroma, excluded from participating in the fullness of the divine life. The bap-

81

tism they practice is "somatic" insofar as it is a physical act, and "psychic" insofar as it conveys "forgiveness of sins." On both levels it remains only the "baptism of John." The eucharist also they celebrate "somatically," eating bread and drinking wine, and "psychically" insofar as they refer these acts to the death of Jesus on Calvary, and celebrate the "forgiveness of sins" procured for them there. Yet their eucharist remains the "passover of the Jews." For they, from the psychic standpoint, are able to perceive divine revelation only insofar as it is mediated to them through actual events. They fail to recognize that these events, perceived from a higher level of insight, themselves are symbols of spiritual processes.

Those who attain to that higher level of insight receive the "baptism of *apolytrōsis*," which is, from one point of view, the reception of the insight (*gnōsis*) itself. Receiving this, they receive the "spirit" which enables them to transcend the psychic topos. Freed from the jurisdiction of the demiurge, they recognize him as an "image" of the Father. They alone celebrate the "divine passover," in the recognition that Jesus' death on the cross symbolizes the revelation of their election. Instead of remaining, like the psychics, excluded from the "fullness" of the divine life, they enjoy and anticipate full communion with the Father.

The whole process of salvation as the psychics experience it, differs qualitatively, then, from that of the pneumatics. Is this "qualitative difference" to be traced to a deterministic soteriology, as Origen claims? Heracleon offers a full description of both the psychic and the pneumatic experience of salvation. In the two conversion stories he exegetes from Jn 4, he shows the origin and nature of the difference between the two "races." To these accounts, then, we now turn.

5. Two Types of Conversion (Jn 4)

Heracleon sets forth his soteriological doctrine most explicitly in his exegesis of the two major conversion stories preserved from his commentary—that of the Samaritan woman in Jn 4.7-42, and that of the centurion's son, which follows in Jn 4.46-54. These two accounts, immediately juxtaposed in the gospel, offer a striking contrast. Heracleon assumes that this effect is intended to show that, in each case, conversion occurs on a fundamentally different level—virtually as a qualitatively different process. He uses the term "pneumatic nature" to characterize the first, and "psychic nature" to characterize the second—terms which seem to justify the assumption of commentators (from Origen to Sagnard) that Heracleon interprets these in terms of his "hypothesis of natures," that is, in terms of a "substantive determinism."

The "centurion's son": an image of psychic salvation

To investigate what these terms mean for Heracleon, we turn first to his exegesis of Jn 4.46 f, which tells of Jesus' healing of the centurion's son. Heracleon recognizes this passage as one that depicts two aspects of conversion. On the one hand, it narrates the son's "healing" from sins through the forgiveness Christ offers; on the other, it relates the father's conversion to faith through the "sign" given in his son's healing.

In many ways, the process of conversion, as Heracleon interprets it here, follows a pattern familiar to us from other Christian writings. The father, although a "basilikos," is himself a "man under authority" (CJ 13.60). Heracleon is referring, clearly, to the parallel accounts in Matthew (8.5-10) and Luke (7.1-10). Heracleon interprets the son's sickness in a moral sense—the sickness is that of "sins." That the son is "near death," Heracleon says, "contradicts the opinion of those who suppose that the soul is immortal" (CJ 13.60). Heracleon (in common with many Christian authors) rejects this commonplace philosophic idea. He cites Mt 10.28 to show that "both the soul and the body" may be destroyed in Gehenna. He goes on to quote 1 Cor 15.53 to show that the soul, although mortal, "has a capacity for salvation when the 'corruptible puts on incorruption,' and the 'mortal puts on immortality,' and 'death is swallowed up in victory.'" But the ruler's son is "about to die," as Heracleon explains from Rom 7.13; the son, having fallen into sins, stands under the law that prescribes death for sins. His father comes to the savior, pleading with him to help his son, and to save him from sins and their penalty, death. The savior, recognizing that the son is incapable of saving himself, "descends to the sick one and heals him from his sickness, that is, from sins; and through the life-giving forgiveness of sins, says, 'your son will live'" (CJ 13.60). His father, hearing these words, "believes" that the savior, not even being present with his son in Capernaum, can heal him. Then his servants come, announcing that the son has recovered at the very moment the savior spoke these words. Then his whole "household" joins the father in believing. Their faith illustrates the savior's words, "unless you see signs and wonders, you do not believe" (Jn 4.48).

So far at least, this description of the process of conversion—a process that turns men from their sins and from death, requiring the forgiveness Christ offers, and faith in him—contains nothing markedly different from many other Christian homilies.

Beyond this, however, what Heracleon explains as its context and meaning marks his viewpoint as unmistakably Valentinian. The ruler, he explains, is not to be taken literally, as a minor official in Judea: on a symbolic level he represents the demiurge. For the ruler, like the demiurge, is "under authority," ruled by others above him. He is called "basilikos" on account of the insignificance and temporality of his authority, "like a minor king set over a small kingdom by a universal king."

That his son is "in Capernaum" also has a specific and symbolic meaning. Heracleon (as noted above, pp. 52 f) takes all the places mentioned in scripture as symbols of different "regions" of spiritual experience. Capernaum in particular signifies the lowest level of existence, i.e., the "extremities of materiality" (CJ 10.11) bordering on primordial chaos. There, "in the lowest part of the mid-region near the sea, that is, in the region immersed in matter," the son lies ill. Who then is this "son"? He is the demiurge's "son," his "own man" (*ho idios autou anthrōpos*), man as created in his image and likeness. And he is "ill," that is, "not in his natural state" (*ou kata physin*, CJ 13. 60). For although he has received from his creator not only the physical vitality of his instinctual life but also the rational and ethical life of his "soul," now, immersed in materiality, he suffers in "ignorance and sins." This condition is critical for him, since as the son of the creator who is also the lawgiver, he stands under the "law of sin and death" (Rom 7.13). Although he still has a "capacity for salvation," his father (who established death as the penalty for sins) cannot violate his own justice to save his own son. So the creator must turn beyond his own power to "the Father of the only savior," asking him to help his son, "that is, this nature." For according to Heracleon, the son represents the *psychic* nature as a whole (CJ 13.60). The savior, responding to the creator's plea, goes to the son and heals him by forgiving his sins, and restoring him to life—to the "eternal life" which is salvation. The creator then "believes," and the angels, "who are the first to see the activities of men in the cosmos," first perceive the son's recovery, and come to him announcing that his son (the "psychic nature") is healed. The angels who are "his household" also come to believe. As Heracleon says, it is characteristic "of all who have this nature"—men, angels, and the creator himself—that they must be persuaded to believe through "deeds and through sense-perception, and not by the logos." The savior is addressing those at the psychic level when he says, "unless you see signs and wonders, you do not believe."

Through this exegesis, Heracleon intends to characterize the process of conversion as the *psychics* experience it. It is only when we turn to his exegesis of another conversion story—which he interprets in a radically different way—that we can grasp how he evaluates the psychic experience of conversion which he has set forth.

The "Samaritan woman": an image of pneumatic redemption

This second conversion story concerns the Samaritan woman who meets Jesus at a well (Jn 4.7 f). This account, placed in conjunction with that of the ruler's son, invites comparison with it—comparison which Heracleon draws to the point of dramatic contrast. The first section of commentary on this story is lost; the extant fragments from Heracleon begin at Jn 4.12. There the woman, having asked where Jesus gets the "living water" of which he speaks, questions whether he is greater than "our father Jacob," who gave the well where "his flocks" are watered. Now the woman has also come there to drink— and this demonstrates, Heracleon says, that

her life and her opinion about it have become temporalized and dried up; for she was worldly (*kosmikē*), and her worldliness is proven by her having come to drink from the well where the flocks of Jacob drink . . . . But the water that the savior gives is of the spirit and his power (CJ 13.10).

What does the Samaritan woman—and her situation of "worldliness"—represent? Heracleon demonstrates (in agreement with parallel gnostic sources[1]) through every detail of his exegesis that she represents the *pneumatic elect*. As the story opens she has lost the vital awareness of her true "life" (*zōē*) —the pneumatic life that emerges in the elect alone (CJ 2.21). She has become "weak and deficient in respect to her life and her conception of it" (CJ 13.10). Out of this weakness she has come to drink from the "well" where "the flocks of Jacob" draw water (cf Jn 4.12).

What is the "well of Jacob"? Janssens claims that for Heracleon it signifies the "life of this world, natural life";[2] others suggest it is the revelation to Israel. I believe neither suggestion is accurate. It is essential to recall that throughout his exegesis Heracleon interprets the figures of Abraham, Moses, and Jacob metaphorically. Each of these figures serves as a variant metaphor for one referent—the demiurge. Which metaphor is used depends on which aspect of the demiurge's activity is being stressed in each case. When he appears as lawgiver and judge, he is represented as Moses (CJ 20.38); when he appears as progenitor of psychic mankind, as the ruler (CJ 13.60) and as the

---

[1] On the equivalence of "Gentile" with "pneumatic," see above, ch. 4 n. 4. On the designation of the "human" element of the seed as "female," see Sagnard, *Gnose*, 552.

[2] Y. Janssens, "L'Episode de la Samaritaine chez Héracléon," *Museon* 62 (1959), 100-151, 277-299.

father Abraham (CJ 20.20) ; when he appears as shepherd, as Jacob (CJ 13.10). Those who are associated with him in all these OT representations, as subjects of his (Moses') jurisdiction, as his (the ruler's) servants, as his (Abraham's) children, and as his (Jacob's) flocks, are represented as those who worship the demiurge, that is, as *psychics.* So when the woman asks whether the savior is greater than "our father Jacob" she intends to ask whether he is greater than the demiurge.

The "well of Jacob" is the place of worship which the demiurge provides for his "sons and his flocks." It symbolizes the religious resources of the psychics. But this "well" offers only "so-called living water" which remains stagnant, and is of limited quantity (CJ 13.10). Its "water" is "perishable" and "susceptible to loss." The Samaritan has been "drinking" from that well; that is, she has been sharing in the worship of psychic Christians. Heracleon says this shows that her own pneumatic "life" and her awareness of it have "dried up." Now the savior comes to offer her "living water" given "from the spirit and his power," life of an entirely different quality:

This life is eternal, not perishing, like the life of the first water which comes from the well; this endures. For the grace and gift of the savior cannot be taken away or used up, and is imperishable for everyone who shares in it (CJ 13.10).

Hearing the savior's offer of "living water," the Samaritan responds with spontaneous recognition, as if hearing what she already has known intuitively. Her answer is "immediate, uncritical, undiscriminating"—a response "appropriate to her nature" (CJ 13.15) since she is already one of those "chosen by the Father." She realizes at once that the psychic worship in which she has been participating is unsatisfying for her. This "water" is only a "reflection, and hard to swallow and unnourishing." She recognizes that she actually "hates the other place," the well of the "so-called living water" (CJ 13.10), and she asks the savior to give her the water of eternal life.

He replies to her request by saying, "go, call your husband, and come here" (Jn 4.16). His apparent refusal to answer seems strange. Heracleon points out that this passage, taken literally, would make no sense. The savior cannot be referring to an ordinary man (*andros kosmikou*), since he knows that (literally speaking) the woman has no husband. In telling her to "call her husband" he is revealing to her that she has a "pleroma," a "husband in the aion," who is her syzygos (CJ

13.11). He calls her to recognize her heavenly counterpart, and in that act of recognition to come from "there," that is, from the psychic topos, to "here," to the pneumatic topos.

In this, Heracleon demonstrates how her experience differs from that of the psychic "centurion's son." The savior could not command the moribund psychic to "live," or to call upon his own resources for "life": the psychic has no such resources (CJ 13.60). In order to be made "alive" he needs to receive the "lifegiving forgiveness of sins." The pneumatic (although her "life" has become "weak and cosmic") is *neither* moribund nor mortal. She has no need of "forgiveness of sins"; she needs only to call upon resources she already has without knowing it. She is to call on her own, unknown "true husband" so that "coming with him to the savior" she may be married by him "into the power and unity and conjunction of her pleroma" (CJ 13.11).

When she first receives the revelation of her pleroma, the woman is bewildered and answers that she has no such "husband." The savior goes on to explain to her that she has had "six men," referring to her involvement in "all material evil" (designated numerologically by the number six; CJ 10.38). She has "whored against reason, acting wantonly" and has been "disgraced and abandoned by them" that is, by the material elements. He explains that none of her involvements with materiality are legitimate or authentic for her. Her own "true husband" is none of these. He is "in the pleroma," her true counterpart even while she has lived with "other men" in ignorance and alienation. So when she desires "living water" of eternal life, the savior turns her to draw upon the hidden resources of pneumatic life that she already has.

Hearing this, she realizes at once the truth of his words, and yet is filled with shame at the disclosure of her "prostitution." Instead of either lying or directly admitting her degradation, she acknowledges the truth discreetly by replying that he must be a prophet, since only a prophet could "know all things" (CJ 13.15). When she asks him the reason for her past shameful involvements, he explains that "through ignorance of God and neglect of his worship and the needs of her own life" she has suffered this alienation. Yet, he adds, she has not come by chance to the well where she could meet him; she has come out of spiritual thirst. Now that she finds the worship of the psychic topos distasteful and unnourishing, she asks him "how and in what way she might be released from prostitution and worship God" (CJ 13.15). She asks whether God should be worshiped "on this mountain" or "in Jerusalem" (Jn 4.20). On the literal level, she seems to be asking about differences in Samaritan and Jewish practice; but Heracleon takes none of these terms literally. He claims that as the woman represents the pneumatic elect, she is speaking on a symbolic level (CJ 13.35). She intends her question to characterize metaphorically the different types of worship she has experienced.

The savior replies with the metaphor of the "places" of worship, to show that there are three kinds of worship that occur on three distinct levels. The first, represented as Mt. Gerizim, occurs at the topos of materiality (*hylē*). This topos belongs to "the devil"; it is "his cosmos," the totality of evil, the "dwelling place of wild animals" (CJ 13.16) This is the realm of mere sense-experience where the passions rage. (Alternatively, it is the region of "sound," purely physical utterance; CJ 6.20.) Those who "live there" are the "pagans," that is, the hylics. Heracleon apparently has in mind (according to the commonplace philosophic critique of pagan religion) the worship of material phenomena. Those who engage in such religion actually worship the "whole material evil" whose principle is the devil.

From the hylic topos, we recall, the psychic nature (the "centurion's son") had to be delivered and restored to the psychic topos ("Jerusalem") where he properly belonged. Here again "Jerusalem" serves as the "image of the psychic topos" (CJ 13.16; cf 10.33). The "Jews" who live there are those who serve the "God of the Jews"; they are the *psychics* who worship the demiurge. The levites among them are "a symbol of those psychics who are found in salvation" (CJ 10.33). When the savior says that Jerusalem is the topos where "the Jews worship," he refers even to Christian worship that occurs on a psychic level. They worship the creator, or rather, "they worship the creation" (CJ 13.19). Heracleon cites Rom 1.25 ("they worship the creation and not the creator") to show that the demiurge is actually only a *creation*, "and not the true creator, who is Christ, since 'all things were made by him, and without him nothing was made' " (CJ 13.19; cf Jn 1.3).[3]

Heracleon goes on to explain that the psychic apprehension of Christ remains on a level of "flesh and error." For they do not see that Christ himself is the creator—and not (as they assume) merely the son of the demiurge. Although salvation emerges from among them ("salvation is of the Jews"), that is, Christ was revealed to the disciples (psychic believers), he has not come to be "in them." In other words, they do not receive the inward and spiritual meaning of the revelation.

[3] Cf Strom 4. (13.) 89-90.

They apprehend only the outward and actual events surrounding Jesus of Nazareth, and they interpret these in the ethical terms that typify the psychic topos. In taking these actual events to be the revelation, they fail to realize that these events are "images of things in the pleroma," that is, symbols of the process of pneumatic redemption. The psychics continue to worship the demiurge "in flesh and error," the one who "is not the Father" but is only his "image" (CJ 13.25).

Those who are pneumatic stand at the third and highest level: they alone perceive the spiritual meaning of those "images" which the psychics mistakenly worship. They recognize the truth—that the demiurge is only the "creation" of Christ and the "image" of the Father. The pneumatics "know whom they worship" and "worship neither the *creation* nor the *creator,* but the Father of truth." They alone worship "in spirit and in truth" (Jn 13.19; Jn 4.22-24).

Now the savior reveals to the Samaritan that she herself is among the pneumatics: he includes her as one who is *"already* a believer" and *"already* numbered among the true worshipers" (CJ 13.16). This explains why she has been frustrated and dissatisfied as long as she remained at the pyschic topos: the erroneous, literal worship of the psychic is alien to her own inner spiritual "life."

This contains a paradox, as Heracleon is well aware. The savior calls on the woman to realize that she has falsely identified herself with her "cosmic" existence, in which she has become "prostituted" to materiality. Her "true nature" is the pneumatic identity given to her as her *pleroma,* which is one with the Father "in spirit and in truth." Her syzygos is of the "pure and invisible divine nature of the Father" (CJ 13.25). Through him she belongs to the Father as one of "his own" (CJ 13.20).

Heracleon can only explain the paradox by acknowledging that those who are pneumatic receive their spiritual identity as the "grace and gift of the savior." The savior acts as agent for the *will of the Father:* and the Father's will is that the pneumatics (*anthrōpoi*) should "know the Father" (CJ 13.38; cf Jn 4.34) and should "worship him" (CJ 13.20; cf Jn 4.23). From her "first formation of genesis" (CJ 2.21) in pre-cosmic election, the pneumatic has a receptive capacity for "eternal life" symbolized in the story by the woman's water jar (CJ 13.31). Although she was unaware of what could "fill" this capacity (having gone to Jacob's well to draw its spiritually unnourishing water), still she has anticipated the coming of one who would offer her the "living water" of pneumatic life. Heracleon notes from this that the "pneumatic ecclesia," i.e., the elect, even in a state of alienation, are marked by such expectation (CJ 13.27). Because the savior perceives in her this receptive capacity and this expectation of his coming, he reveals himself to her (CJ 13.28). The revelation of the Father's will in election "enlightens" the pneumatic and culminates in her "marriage" as a member of the elect with her divine syzygos: the savior restores the two into union (CJ 13.11).

Heracleon's description of this process deserves close attention, especially from those who interpret his teaching as one of "natural salvation." Irenaeus, for example, takes the "doctrine of syzygies" as evidence that the Valentinians consider themselves "naturally" identical with divine being. He says the Valentinians teach that "we (psychics) have grace for use, so that it will again be taken from us; but they themselves have grace as their own special possession, which has descended from above by reason of an ineffable and indescribable syzygos" (AH 1.6.4). Irenaeus supports his inference by pointing out that the Valentinians regard moral effort as irrelevant and unnecessary for pneumatics.

Heracleon uses the syzygos metaphor, on the contrary, to express not a theology of identification but a theology of election. It is true that the redemption of the elect (depending as it does on the will of the Father alone) is, so to speak, inevitable. Yet those who are of the elect are anything but "naturally spiritual" in their existential condition. Heracleon describes the woman who represents the elect as having been "destroyed in the deep matter of error" (CJ 13.20). As ignorant of God as of her own nature, she has neglected both, and is shown as having violated reason. She is tormented by doubt and ignorance, torn by conflicting passions. The savior's message is not that this destroyed human being is simply, in herself, "of divine nature"—far from it.

What the savior reveals is that she has already been given a pneumatic identity of which she is ignorant, one that is her authentic "spiritual fulfillment" (*plērōma*). It is not she "herself" who is revealed to be in union with the Father, but her *pleroma,* whom she must come to recognize as an essential part of her own "true identity" (*idian perigraphēn,* CJ 2.21). He is, so to speak, her "ecstatic identity," her "life hid with Christ in God" (Col 3.3). She must cast off the passions of her false relationships and come to the savior, to be with him married "in power and union and conjunction with her pleroma" (CJ 13.11).

As she receives the revelation of gnosis, she receives her "heavenly bridegroom": the moment she receives it is the moment of her "mar-

91

riage" (CJ Frag 45; AH 1.21.4). The reception of this gnosis may also be enacted in the sacrament of *apolytrōsis* (also called the "bride-chamber"; see above, pp. 78 f) in which the celebrant speaks as the savior who unites two in marriage (CJ 13.11; cf AH 1.13.3). We can see now how strikingly appropriate are the liturgical words Irenaeus relates: "I *will* for you to share in my *grace,* since the Father of all beholds your angel (syzygos) in his presence . . . ." The recipient, as the bride, receives and *becomes* her heavenly bridegroom. Another parallel to this liturgy occurs in Heracleon's interpretation of Jn 2.1-11 as an allegory of the divine marriage. Although much of his exegesis of this passage is lost, his view that the wine miracle symbolizes the transformation of the human into the divine concurs with the liturgical act Irenaeus describes (AH 1.13.1; see above, pp. 79 f). The Valentinians apparently understand the pneumatic marriage as a reality already present for the elect.

Two "standpoints" in relation to the pneumatic "marriage"

What of the psychics? Are they excluded from receiving gnosis, from participating in the "marriage"? Heracleon answers that they *are* excluded, at least for the present. He shows how the experience of the pneumatic differs from that of the psychics when he interprets Jn 4. 31-38. This passage describes that when the woman departs to re-enter the city, the disciples return to the savior. For Heracleon they represent the psychic level of the majority of Christians. Their understanding (and that of the Christian community they founded) is "carnal" (*sarkic,* CJ 13.35). They come "wanting to commune with him" (CJ 13.32), and yet they were absent from the savior's revelation to the pneumatic ecclesia. They are compared to the "foolish virgins" of Mt 25. As those virgins, having gone out to buy the oil they lacked, missed the bridegroom's coming, so the disciples, having gone "into the cosmos" to buy bread, missed the "marriage." In their concern for what is immediately sense-perceptible—oil for their lamps and bread to eat—both have neglected the savior, who is the true light and the true bread (CJ 13.32). The disciples and the foolish virgins are both excluded from the "wedding."

Behind this fragment of exegesis, as R. Staats points out, stands a Valentinian tradition of interpreting the parable of Mt 25 with reference to the contrast between psychic and pneumatic modes of perception.[4] According to this tradition, the five "foolish virgins" symbolize the five bodily senses which serve perception at the psychic topos. Alternatively, they symbolize the virtues which characterize the psychics—faith, love, grace, peace, and hope. The five "wise virgins" represent the five modes of "rational perception" (logikē aisthēsis), as well as the powers of the pneumatics—insight (gnōsis), understanding, obedience, patience, and mercy.[5] The "wise virgins" are, according to this tradition, all themselves pneumatic "brides," all having their syzygies as their given "husbands." The foolish virgins who represent the psychics are (as in Heracleon's exegesis) excluded from the wedding.

In Heracleon's exegesis (as in Valentinian exegesis in general, cf AH 3.1 f) the disciples exemplify this psychic level of perception. They understand nothing of the revelation of the "marriage." Although they desire to commune with the savior, all they can offer him is "what they bought in Samaria," that is, in the cosmos. They offer Jesus ordinary food, and when he replies that he has food they know nothing about, they wonder whether someone has brought him a meal! The savior answers by explaining to them that he is speaking in metaphor. To show them "what he intends with the woman," he explains that his "food" is to do the Father's will; and the Father wills "for men (anthrōpous) to know the Father and be saved" (CJ 13.38).

For Heracleon, this expression of the Father's will does not mean that the savior comes to save "mankind" as a whole. He interprets the term anthrōpos technically (see above, pp. 33 f) to designate the elect who participate in the aion Anthropos, the pleromic syzygos of Ecclesia (CJ 2.21). To save the elect, the savior has come into "Samaria, that is, into the cosmos." To accomplish this work is "his food and his rest and his power."

How then can the psychics be saved? Heracleon indicates that although excluded from the present celebration of the marriage, the psychics' rejection is neither total nor final. The pneumatic ecclesia—having shared in the "marriage"—now turns toward the psychics to share the revelation with them. As the savior enlightens the pneumatic ecclesia, so its members are to enlighten the psychics. When the savior says that he is the "light of the cosmos" (cf Jn 8.12), he means that he enlightens the "cosmos" (ornament) of the cosmos, that is,

[4] R. Staats, "Die törichten Jungfrauen von Matthäus 25 in gnostischer und anti-gnostischer Literatur," Christentum und Gnosis, ed. W. Eltester (Berlin, 1969), 98 f.

[5] "Die törichten Jungfrauen," 102.

the *elect;* but when he tells the elect that *they* are the light of the cosmos (cf Mt 5.14), he means that they are "the light of those who are *psychic*" (CJ 6.59-60). Heracleon sees the same principle expressed in the account of Jn 4.28. The Samaritan, having received "living water," leaves her water jar (that is, her "disposition and intuition" of the pneumatic life, CJ 13.31) with the savior, and immediately goes back "into the cosmos, preaching to the called the presence of Christ." For it is "through the spirit and by the spirit" (the pneumatic ecclesia) that "the soul" (the psychic nature) "is led to the savior" (CJ 13.31).

Heracleon often warns pneumatics against asserting their superiority over psychics. He says they are not to keep for themselves the gifts of divine grace they receive, but to "pour them out" for "the eternal life of others" (CJ 13.10). The allegory of the cleansing of the temple (Jn 2.12 f; see above, p. 67) also serves to warn the elect against thinking of the pneumatic gifts in terms of their own advantage, instead of recognizing them as a grace freely given, and giving them freely in turn to the psychics. The story of the Samaritan concludes by relating that she, as the "chosen, single in form and unique," goes to preach to "the called" who are "the many." By her testimony "many psychics" are drawn "out of the city, that is, out of the cosmos" (CJ 13.51) toward the savior.

The psychics who come to the savior apprehend him only partially, at least in the present age. Instead of receiving his direct revelation, they must first receive it through the human witness of the elect (CJ 13.53). Even when they meet with him, he is "among them" but not "within them," indicating that they can perceive him only externally without discerning his presence within themselves (CJ 13.51). Their relationship with him is limited not only in quality but also in duration; he remains among them "for two days"; during the time he spends with them he greatly increases them in faith through his own word; then he is "separated from them" (CJ 13.52). Heracleon says that the "two days" signify either the present age and the age to come, or alternatively, the time before the passion and the time after it. He also explains that the first "day" is *hylic* and the second *psychic* (CJ 10.37); so the "two days" may symbolize the transition from the hylic to the psychic topos, the transition that the centurion's son has undergone (CJ 13.60). In the present age, the psychic Christian apprehends the savior only from the limited standpoint of the psychic topos.

But the psychics anticipate another stage of transition: they look forward to the "age to come" which is to be the "rest in the marriage"

(CJ 10.19; 13.52). They expect to be present at this "feast" which follows upon the end of "this age." Heracleon infers from Jn 2.9—the story of the marriage at Cana—that their archetype, the demiurge, is to preside as "master of the feast." But after the banquet the demiurge is to be excluded from the consummation of the marriage; he will not be allowed to enter into the "bridechamber" of the pleroma. He is represented as the "bridegroom's friend" (Jn 3.29) who stands outside the door of the bridechamber and, hearing the bridegroom's voice, rejoices with him. This is the "fullness of joy" for the demiurge, and his "repose" (CJ Frag 45; Exc 65.1-2; cf Jn 3.29).

Are the psychics who attain salvation destined to be excluded, with the demiurge, from the consummation of the divine marriage? The accounts of Irenaeus, Hippolytus, and Theodotus indicate that Valentinian eschatology clearly differentiates between the final destiny of the psychic and the pneumatic elements (*psychika*/*pneumatika*). These sources agree that it is impossible for the psychic element (*to psychikon*) to gain access to the pleroma (cf AH 1.7.1; Exc 63 f). Only the pneumatic element (*to pneumatikon*) may enter there. Are these excluded elements (*psychika*) identical with the psychics *themselves* (*psychikoi*), those persons who stand at the psychic topos in the present age? On this point the sources apparently disagree.[6] Irenaeus claims that they *are* identical and therefore that all who are *psychics* are excluded from the pleroma (AH 1.7.1).

Evidence from Theodotus and from Heracleon suggests that, on the contrary, the excluded psychic elements (*psychika*) are *not* identical with the psychics *themselves* (*psychikoi*). In the present age, pneumatics as well as psychics wear "souls" (*psychas*) as their cosmic "garments" (AH 1.6.1; 1.7.1; Exc 63.1). That these "psychic garments" are excluded from the pleroma does not necessarily mean that the psychics themselves are excluded; I believe the evidence indicates that they are not. *All* who are finally reunited with the Father, pyschics and pneumatics alike, must "put off" the psychic elements before they can enter his presence.

While pneumatics can receive the "perfection" of the "marriage" already in the cosmos, the psychics who are saved must await their perfection as an eschatological event. They remain "psychic," imperfect, "until the consummation" (Exc 62-63). Only then will the ecclesia itself become complete, and consist of both "the elect and the called"

---

[6] Sagnard, *Gnose*, 387 f, attempts to reconcile these differences in favor of Irenaeus' version.

(Exc 58.1). Theodotus offers what is lacking in the extant fragments of Heracleon—a full description of the reunion of both the elect and the called into one ecclesia.

Theodotus explains that, at the end of this age, "all who are saved," psychics and pneumatics alike, will pass beyond the cosmos into the ogdoad. There they will celebrate the "marriage feast" of the ecclesia and the savior. At the "great feast" (CJ 10.19) psychics and pneumatics will rejoice together, all alike wearing as "wedding garments" their "souls" (*psychas*) which signify their communality (Exc 63.1-2). The feast will continue "until all are equal and know each other": until all enter into equal and mutual relationship. Then the pneumatic elements (apparently of *all* participants in the feast, since the distinctions between those formerly "psychic" and "pneumatic" shall have been obliterated) divest themselves of their *souls*. The psychic elements of all must be discarded, and these "garments" remain outside the pleroma with the demiurge who bestowed them. All those who enter the pleroma are now transformed into "noetic aions" as they pass into the "bridechamber" (Exc 64). Heracleon says that the entrance into the pleroma initiates the "third day" which is pneumatic, and signifies the "resurrection of the ecclesia" (CJ 10.37). It cannot be the elect, the *pneumatic ecclesia,* who are "resurrected," for, according to Valentinian symbology, they who are the "living" were never "dead." The psychics, who in this age are the "dead," are promised resurrection (CJ 13.66). When it occurs they undergo a *second* transition, this time from the psychic to the pneumatic topos. They become transformed so that they, as members of the total ecclesia, may participate with the elect in "eternal life."

Irenaeus gives a very different picture of this process. Unlike Theodotus, he describes the pneumatic marriage not as an *inclusive* process but as an *exclusive* one. He omits any reference to the equalization process Theodotus describes, and implies instead that it is the *psychics themselves* (*psychikoi*), rather than the *souls* of both psychics and pneumatics alike (*psychika*), that remain outside the pleroma. Detailed examination of these texts must be deferred to a forthcoming article.[7] Here I suggest only that the version Irenaeus gives in AH 1.7.1 betrays polemical distortion, while Theodotus' version concurs with Irenaeus' own statements in AH 1.6 and 8, and with the evidence from Heracleon.

[7] E. Pagels, "Conflicting Versions of Valentinian Eschatology: Irenaeus' Treatise vs. the Excerpts from Theodotus."

Like Theodotus, Heracleon indicates that, having undergone the first transition, those Christians who are now "psychic" are to undergo in the future the second transformation. In that future transformation, the limits of their present apprehension of Christ will be overcome; then they "no longer" will need human witness to believe in the savior, but will themselves receive direct revelation from "the truth itself" (CJ 13.53).

The contrast between the conversion of the centurion's son and the redemption of the Samaritan woman shows how the experience of psychics and pneumatics *in the cosmos* differs qualitatively. The psychic, as the "called," can never achieve in the present the certainty of his salvation. He is "immersed in materiality" and in "sins." For him this condition is potentially fatal; he stands under the demiurge's law that prescribes death for sins. To be delivered from death, he needs the "life-giving forgiveness of sins." He must have faith, but his faith is directed specifically toward the "psychic Christ" whose death on the cross ensures his "forgiveness." Receiving this, he is transferred from the hylic to the psychic topos, and must then persevere "by choice" in "good works" in order to receive "salvation" as his "reward."

The pneumatic, as the "chosen," receives even in this world an utterly "certain" and "imperishable" redemption. Even while she remains ignorant of her pneumatic "life" and seems to suffer total destruction in materiality, her "life" cannot be extinguished or lost. The Father has already chosen her as one of "his own," bestowing election as a "gift of grace" poured down "from above." She encounters the savior as the pneumatic revealer who discloses to her her own hidden, divine pleroma. Through his words she spontaneously comes to recognize that her own "true nature" is essentially one with the "divine nature of the Father." As she receives this gnosis, she participates in the joy of the "divine marriage" even as she remains in the cosmos.

These differences between the experience of the pneumatics and of the psychics who are saved are sustained only in the *oikonomia*. As long as they remain in the cosmos, the situation and role of each remain distinct. The pneumatic ecclesia becomes in the cosmos the means of evangelizing the psychics, so that those who attain salvation may finally come to share in the reunion of the total ecclesia, consisting of the "elect and the called," with the father. What the pneumatics experience as a present reality, the psychic Christians only anticipate as a future hope.

97

6. Valentinian Anthropology: "Generation" (Jn 8) and "Seed" (Jn 4.35 f)

The claim that the Valentinians teach a theology of election raises an immediate and obvious objection: when they refer to three human "natures" (hylic/psychic/pneumatic), aren't they using the language of *determinism?* When they describe how these "natures" originate, through the metaphors of generation, expressed either in social terms (father/son/child) or in biological ones (sperm/offspring) —does not their selection of terms clearly indicate that they are presupposing a kind of "natural determinism"?

Two interpretations: "determinism" and "free will"

The above interpretation has been taken for granted in the majority of recent studies of gnosticism. Förster interprets the Valentinian description of the three "natures" as the designation of natural categories.[1] Bultmann takes up this assumption, claiming that the Valentinians teach natural determinism, so that "redemption occurs as a great natural process . . . the destiny of the soul is determined through its nature." Valentinian anthropology excludes human freedom and

[1] *Valentin,* 28 f; 22-23: "The total being (*Wesen*) of the pneumatic is a natural 'given' that cannot by any means be changed, not even through sin."

human choice: "Faith is not genuine decision, but recognition of one's own mythical origin . . . the gnostic is one who is already 'saved by nature' and the unbeliever is on the basis of his evil nature (*physis*) already lost." [2] Similarly, throughout his comprehensive study of Valentinian theology, Sagnard assumes that the "law of three substances" defines three distinct, predetermined human "natures." Valentinian theology differs from Paul's (according to Sagnard) in that Paul thinks that human beings *receive* the capacity to participate in the divine life, while the Valentinians consider that the pneumatics "already have" such participation as an "actual natural possession of divine life." [3]

This view, of course, has not originated with contemporary scholars. It claims the authorization of the 2nd/3rd-century heresiologists, especially of Irenaeus, Clement, and Origen, who agree that the Valentinians teach that souls are "naturally" predestined to salvation or destruction. Clement says that they teach that some are "saved natures," saved "of necessity" by a presumed "natural affinity with God." Others are "lost natures," who have no possibility of salvation (Exc 56.3; Strom 4.89). A third type of "nature" is able to choose salvation "by learning and purification and doing good works" (Strom 2.[2.]10-11). Irenaeus and Origen also assume that the Valentinian "hypothesis concerning different natures" is a clearly deterministic doctrine (AH 1.6.1-2; CJ 2.13; 20.20-24; Prin 3.4 f).

Langerbeck and Schottroff, challenging this view in 1967 and 1969, have offered an opposite interpretation of Valentinian anthropology. They suggest that the interpretation of the *physis* language as "deterministic" actually *caricatures* gnostic anthropology. They claim that this polemical caricature has been mistaken by historians for a description. Schottroff concludes from her analysis that the terminology of the three "natures," far from assuming a substantive determinism that excludes free will, is intended to describe the different modes of human existence as they are constituted by free will. She declares that

Hyle, psyche, and *pneuma* are definitions of being (*Wesen/ousia*) that describe the being of mankind in relation to the poles of the dualism—to salvation and perdition . . . . Each person who is to be saved is defined through *hyle, psyche,* and *pneuma* . . . . The pneumatic is not exempted from the role of the psychic: he must decide himself on the basis of free will for salvation or perdition. [4]

[2] *Evangelium des Johannes,* 21-24; see also 96 f, 114, 240.
[3] *Gnose,* 387-415, 567-68, 606-7.
[4] "Animae," 92-93; see also Langerbeck, *Aufsätze,* 38 f.

Investigation of Heracleon's Johannine exegesis indicates that to analyze gnostic anthropology in terms of *either* of these alternatives proves misleading. The philosophic question of determinism and free will is not the issue that motivates the development of gnostic anthropology. As Quispel has suggested, the Valentinian description of the "natures" emerges instead from a theology of election.[5] More specifically, the Valentinians have developed their description of the hylic, psychic, and pneumatic "natures" (as they themselves claim[6]) as an exegetical interpretation of Johannine and Pauline election theology.[7]

To investigate how Heracleon actually uses the terminology of the three "natures" and the correlated metaphors of "generation" and "seed," we turn first to his exegesis of Jn 8 (which concerns primarily the psychics) and secondly to his exegesis of Jn 4.35 f (which concerns the elect).

The story of the centurion's son has shown the demiurge represented as the "father" of the "psychic nature," while that of the Samaritan woman has shown the "Father of truth" revealed as "Father" of the "pneumatic nature" (see above, p. 90). The devil is also represented as a "natural father," but only of those who are of "hylic nature" (CJ 20.20-24; 20.28). In Heracleon's exegesis of Jn 8 the generation metaphor recurs in similar terms. There the savior, speaking to "the Jews," receives from the crowd three distinct types of response. Heracleon refers each type of response to the generation of the respondants from three different "fathers"—the devil (cf Jn 8.44), the demiurge ("Abraham," Jn 8.33 f), and the "Father of the savior" (Jn 8.18 f). The savior goes on to say that those who are "children of (his) Father" love him ("if God were your Father you would love me,"Jn 8.42) and hear him ("he who is of God hears the words of God," Jn 8.47). Those who hate him and do not hear him are "of (their) father the devil" (Jn 8.44). Still others neither hear nor love him at first, but take an indeterminate position. The savior offers these the possibility

[5] G. Quispel, "La conception de l'homme dans la gnose valentinienne" (Eranos Jahrbuch 1947), 262, 274-275: "Valentinian gnosticism is a mysticism (*mystique*) that places the emphasis on grace and election . . . . The Valentinians considered the 'spirit' which they had received not as a natural endowment, but as a gift of grace."

[6] Cf AH 1.1.3; 1.8.1-4; 4.6.1 f.

[7] Langerbeck, *Aufsätze*, 79: "The starting point of Valentinus is not a supernaturally revealed gnosis that comes onto the one who has received the 'spirit' in the sense of a mysterious metaphysical substance . . . . His starting point is the NT (especially the Pauline and Johannine) conception of election, which is the Christian meaning of the representation of Israel as the chosen 'seed of Abraham.' "

of coming to hear his word and to love him (Jn 8:31-33) . Heracleon concludes that these are "children of Abraham," that is, of the demiurge. They are psychics, and (like the centurion's son) have a "capacity for salvation" (CJ 13.60) so that they may come to faith and truth.

Heracleon interprets the savior's saying to the psychics ("if you are children of Abraham, you do the works of Abraham," Jn 8.39) by taking Jn 8.41 ("you do the works of your father") as a general principle. What are the "works of Abraham" that the psychics are to do? He answers from Jn 8.56 that the "work" of "Abraham" is that he "rejoiced to see" the savior's coming. Heracleon's interpretation of "Abraham" as the demiurge virtually requires that his "work" consists in the act of faith, since the demiurge does no "work" in an ethical sense. Heracleon states that "faith is a work," finding support for this interpretation in Rom 4.3, where Paul says that "Abraham" (the demiurge) "believed God, and it was accounted to him for righteousness" (CJ 20.10; 13.60) . Valentinian exegesis of Romans (cited in Origen's Romans commentary) offers a parallel exegesis. There "Abraham" (the demiurge) and the "children of Abraham" (the psychics), also called "the circumcised" and "the Jews," are said to be justified "from faith" (CR 5.8; cf Rom 3.30) . Nevertheless this "faith" requires an act of repentance; it is a "work" that psychics must confirm by other works. Those who believe and who persevere in both the "work" of faith and other "good works" attain salvation as their "due reward." In Paul's words, "to one who works, his wages are not reckoned as a gift but as his due" (Rom 4.2; CR 6.6) .

Heracleon goes on to explain that there are some among "the Jews" whom the savior addresses in Jn 8 who are *not* "Abraham's," that is, they are not of psychic nature. These are children, not of the demiurge, but of the "unbegotten Father." Although they remain among "the Jews" and are "called seed of Abraham," these are not psychics. For psychics are "Jews openly," but these are "Jews in secret" (Rom 2. 28 f) . Recognizing this, the savior acknowledges that they, like himself, are "of the Father." He says to them, "what I have seen with my Father I speak, and what you have heard from your Father you do" (Jn 8.38) . Heracleon takes this to mean that they are pneumatics (an exegesis that again is paralleled in the Valentinian commentary on Rom 2.29-31; CR 168.15) . He explains that the Father himself has communicated with them as he has with the savior. Referring to Jn 6.45 ("everyone who has heard from the Father and has learned comes to me") , Herac-

leon says that such persons have "learned from the Father before coming into birth." He sees them as having been "generated from" the
Father, citing such passages as Jn 8.42 and 47. Alternatively, they can
be described as having been "drawn" by the Father (Jn 6.44) and
"chosen" by him (Jn 15.16). These are the savior's "own" who "hear
his words" (Jn 10.27; 8.47) and love him (Jn 8.42).

There are also some present who cannot hear the savior's words because they "are not of God" (Jn 8.47). Heracleon says that

the reason they can neither hear the word of Jesus nor understand his speech
is given in the saying, "you are of the father of the devil," meaning, "of the
being (ousia) of the devil," which reveals to them at last their own nature
(physis), that is, that they had been preelected (proelēsas) neither to be
children of Abraham . . . nor of God (CJ 20.8).

Heracleon stresses that Jn 8.44 shows that those addressed are "of the
being (ousia) of the devil" (CJ 20.20; 20.23-24), to show that these are
hylics, "those who are sons of the devil by nature (physei)."

Confronted with this exegesis, Origen insists on a deterministic interpretation of Heracleon's words: "Now it is clear that they say that some
men are of the same nature as the devil, and others of other natures,
which they call psychic and pneumatic" (CJ 20.20). Origen replies
to Heracleon's "determinism" by stating that "those who do not understand what is meant by the term 'seed' (sperma) and the term 'child'
(teknon) regard the two as equivalent." He says they fail to see that
the first term expresses potentiality and the other actuality. Failing
to recognize this, such persons fail to distinguish between the term
"seed of Abraham" and the term "child of Abraham." Such exegetes
(Origen continues) claim that when the savior speaks to "the Jews"
he addresses those who are "seed of Abraham," genetically characterized as such by "spermatic logoi" which they receive from their
"father" (that is, from the demiurge). Those receiving his "seed,"
according to the Valentinian hypothesis (as Origen represents it) "grow
naturally (physei) into children of Abraham." Whoever is not born
with this seed in him cannot become the "child of Abraham." (CJ
20.2). Origen believes that the same applies to those generated from
the devil (who are "naturally lost") and to those generated from God:

Those who introduce the mythopoetics about different natures (physeis) and
say that they are by nature (physei) and from the first (ek prōtes) sons of
God, think that they are receptive to the words of God only through their
genetic affinity (syngenēs) with him (CJ 20.33).

The "adoption" of psychics "by choice" and "by merit"

Those commentators who take Origen's interpretation at face value (as do Förster and Sagnard[8]) miss not only his polemical bias but also the flaws in his argument. First, Heracleon clearly states that the filial terminology does not always designate a determinative "natural relationship." He declares that, on the contrary, such terminology may bear no less than three possible meanings. First, it may designate a relationship constituted "by nature" (*physei*); secondly, a relationship constituted "by choice" (*gnomē*); third, one constituted "by merit" (*axia*). The relationship of "nature" involves one being "generated from" another, whose "son" he is "in the proper sense of the word." Besides this "natural" relationship, there is another form of relationship constituted "by adoption" (*thesis*). This second type of filiation occurs through "choice," as "when someone who does the will of another by his own choice is called the child of the one whose will he does." Alternatively, it occurs by "merit" when one "does the deeds of another, and is called the son of the one whose deeds he promotes." Both forms of adoptive relationship depend on the initiative of the would-be "son" (and not of the father he chooses). Heracleon says that such adoptive relationship (which is constituted either through choice or through action) is available to the psychics (CJ 20.24). Although they are "children of Abraham" (the demiurge) "by nature," their "nature" conveys no predetermined destiny. As Irenaeus says, they stand midway between the pneumatic and the hylic elements (AH 1.6.1). Valentinian sources describe their dual potential through the myth of the demiurge. They say that the demiurge, "father" of the psychics, came from the *epistrophē*, that is, from the moment of transition, the conversion from hyle, which is a "turning toward" the pneumatic topos (AH 1.4.5; Ref 32.6-7). The psychics are those who stand at this "turning point" which is their standpoint (*topos*) in the cosmos. Clement says that "the psychic element, being self-constituting (*autexousion on*) has the capacity either for faith and immortality or for unbelief and destruction, according to its own choice" (Exc 56.3). Heracleon says that psychics can choose to become by adoption either "sons of the devil" or "sons of God" (CJ 20.24). Their choice reconstitutes their nature, directs them either into "evil" or "good works," and decides their eternal destiny.

Heracleon cites as evidence for their situation the words Jesus ad-

---

[8] Förster, *Valentin*, 28 f; Sagnard, *Gnose*, 503 f.

dresses to the psychics (to "the Jews who had believed in him," Jn 8.
31). The savior offers them salvation—not an *assurance* of it, but the
prospect of it, contingent on their present choice and future action:
"if you remain in my word, you are truly my disciples, and you shall
know the truth, and the truth shall make you free." He sets the alternatives before them: they can either become slaves to sin (to the devil)
and perish; or they can choose to become sons of God and attain
eternal life (cf Jn 8.34-36).

The psychics' capacity to decide their final destiny has often been
described as their "free will" (so Clement, above; also Brooke, Henrici,
Sagnard, Schottroff[9]). Heracleon himself never uses this term. He
shows that the psychics do experience a range of "choice" between salvation and destruction, but their "choice" is not the power to constitute themselves; it is not "free will" (*autexousia*) in the proper sense
of the word. This philosophic term, applied to Heracleon's doctrine,
proves to be anachronistic and misleading. The conditions of psychic
existence and of their "choice" are constituted for them by the demiurge. Their "choice," in fact their only option, is whether to obey
the will of the Father or the will of the devil.

"Natural generation" as election: the pneumatic "seed"

Hylics and pneumatics have no such choice. They are already the
"natural" sons of the devil or of God. The biological metaphor is
meant to show that their affinity (whether with God or the devil)
occurs (like natural, biological sonship) prior to, and apart from, any
choice or activity on the son's part. Therefore the pneumatics do "the
will of the Father" spontaneously (CJ 20.20) since he has willed to
elect them (CJ 13.38). Those who are "naturally" sons of the devil can
be described in equivalent terms as those "pre-elected" to belong to
him (CJ 20.20). As pneumatics have not chosen God, but are "chosen"
by him (Jn 15.16), so the hylics have neither choice nor will of their
own (CJ 20.20). Apparently the Valentinians have concluded that the
doctrine of election to grace necessarily is correlated with a doctrine of
election to reprobation. Those who are elected to reprobation are
"naturally incapable" of apprehending faith and truth (CJ 20.28).
Their situation is exactly opposite to that of those elected to grace,

[9] Brooke, *Fragments*, 45 f; G. Henrici, *Valentinianische Gnosis und die Heilige Schrift* (Berlin, 1877), 23 f; Sagnard, *Gnose*, 512-516; Schottroff, "Animae," 85 f.

whose "nature" consists of divine "spirit and truth" (CJ 13.25) : the hylics' nature consists of demonic "error and falsehood" (CJ 20.28) .

To describe the origin of the pneumatic elect, on the other hand, Valentinian theologians frequently use the metaphor of the "seed." Heracleon's discussion of the "seed" focuses on his exegesis of Jn 4.35-38. There the savior offers to his disciples (i.e., to psychics, see p. 92) the parable of the seed and the harvest. According to Heracleon, the savior intends for this parable to explain to psychics why the "woman" —the pneumatic ecclesia—can "commune with him" while they are excluded.

The "harvest" Jesus describes contradicts the disciples' understanding of it. They expect it to occur in the future ("in four months," CJ 13.41) . They regard themselves (the disciples) as the "sowers" (CJ 13.50) . Apparently their interpretation is the one Matthew gives of the parable of the sower (Mt 13.18-23) : the "seed" is the word of the preaching; Christ and the apostles are the "sowers"; the "harvest" of believers, the result of the preaching, is expected in the future, when the word has grown and "born fruit" in the hearers.

Heracleon explicitly refers to this interpretation of the harvest parable, which he apparently considers valid only within the psychic framework. In terms of Valentinian theology, the Matthean interpretation could apply only to the process of conversion at the *psychic* level. Heracleon places this psychic interpretation in relation to an alternative pneumatic interpretation. At this higher level, each term of the parable serves to describe the process by which the *pneumatics* experience redemption. For in this case the "sowing" refers not to the word of preaching, but to the elect themselves, sown as the "pneumatic seed." So also the "sowing" does not occur in the present, anticipating a future harvest (as the apostles preach in the present, and expect the "fruit" of their efforts to come in the future) . Instead the "sowing" has already taken place, and the "harvest" is present even now (CJ 13.41) .

Pointing out how the savior reverses the expected sequence of events, Heracleon interprets the parable as an allegory of the election. Only by recognizing that the sowing has *already* occurred can one understand the readiness of the pneumatic "seed" for the "harvest," i.e., the ecclesia's present receptiveness to the savior. How was the seed sown, if not through the apostolic preaching? Heracleon explains that it must have been sown *before* the present age, before the cosmos, so that the savior finds the "harvest" ready for him. The savior says himself that he is not the sower but the reaper (CJ 13.46) :

For the first one began the sowing, and the second one the reaping. Both could not have begun at the same time. It was necessary first to have been sown, and then later to have been reaped. When the sower has ceased to sow, then the reaper reaps (CJ 13.49).

Who, if not the savior, has done the "sowing"? Heracleon explains that the sower is the one *prior* to the savior who comes into the world. The sower is called "son of man," but specifically distinct from the savior "who is also called son of man." It is that "son of man beyond the topos" (CJ 13.49) who sows, the one who (as other Valentinian accounts describe) has united with Sophia to sow the "seed" secretly into those who are later created in the cosmos. The "seed" (the elect) are sown "by another." They receive from the logos their "first formation of origin" through this sowing. Then later the logos, coming into the cosmos as the savior, encounters the "seed," lost and alienated there, and "brings and reveals to them their original form· and enlightenment, and their own definition" (CJ 2.21).

Irenaeus relates that the "seed" is sown into the cosmos through the unwitting agency of the demiurge (AH 2.19.1-8). The means of this sowing are (as Heracleon agrees) the "angels of the oikonomia," through whom "as means" the seed are sown and raised in cosmic existence. The angels are those who the savior says "have labored" over the harvest, having sown "in weeping and sweat and labor" to prepare the "chosen ground" and to raise it to maturity (CJ 13.50).

Once the seed has been raised to ripeness, Heracleon says, the savior comes "as reaper," and sends his "angels" as reapers to harvest the seed. Although these are called "angels," Heracleon explains that they are actually the heavenly counterparts (or syzygies) of the elect on earth. In the "harvest," each is sent "to his own soul" (CJ 13.49).

In this we can recognize the affinity between Heracleon's teaching on the "seed" and the doctrine of the "spiritual seed" familiar to us from other accounts of Valentinian doctrine. To explore the numerous parallels is a task beyond our present scope. As Sagnard has said, however, this doctrine of the spiritual seed, the "grace-given element of election," forms the primary theme of Valentinian theology. Irenaeus' account takes up this theme especially in AH 1.5.6–1.7.5, where the origin, development, "formation," "perfection," and "consummation" of the seed are described in successive stages. These stages proceed like an organic process of growth. According to his account, the seed (as it appears in the cosmos) has originated in a secret "deposit" of it within those "chosen." Before the creation of the cosmos, the seed was produced by Sophia, in her kenomic exile (AH 1.4.5–1.5.1) where she experienced the longing for the coming of the "light." Beholding the light of the "angels" who accompany the savior, she conceives the seed "in their image." Yet what she conceives is "unformed, without species, and imperfect" (AH 2.19.1). Christ, coming into the kenoma, first separates the "pneumatic element" which includes Sophia and the seed, from the "passions," offering to her and the seed the "first formation of genesis." The seed, still in need of the "second formation of gnosis," then is deposited "by an ineffable providence" into the cosmos which the demiurge created (AH 1.5.6). The deposited seed, through the agency of the demiurge, thereby is "sown" into the "souls" of human beings he creates in the cosmos (AH 2.19.2). Sown in a state of "infancy," that is, of potentiality, the seed is to develop in the cosmos into maturity, until it becomes "ready and ripe" to receive "the perfect logos," who will bring it into the "form of gnosis" (AH 2.19. 4). Heracleon's doctrine of the seed's origin demonstrates that he perceives the psychic and pneumatic as qualitatively different. The task of the pneumatic "seed" in the cosmos, he says, is both to "educate" those who are psychic, and lead them to salvation, and also to become "educated" themselves into the awareness of their own maturity or "perfection" (teleiōsis). That "perfection" consists in attaining "gnosis" (AH 1.6.1-2). When this process is completed, those psychics who have been saved through the agency of the elect attain to their own "salvation and rest" outside the pleroma. The "whole seed," when it is perfected, finally attains to reintegration and reunion with the Father within the pleroma (AH 1.7.1).

This theme of the elect seed also dominated the Excerpts that Clement preserves. As Sagnard says of the Excerpts as a whole, "despite distinctions of schools, the same essence of Valentinian gnosticism, and even, doubtless, of gnosticism in general," consists in the doctrine that the divine pneuma has been deposited "as seed" in the elect, to develop throughout earthly existence, and to reascend finally to the "fullness" of divine life.[10]

It is striking to note that although the doctrine of the seed forms the central theme of his theology as well, Heracleon, by contrast with Ptolemy and Theodotus, alludes to the myth of its pre-cosmic origin only in passing. In the passage above he refers to it only to explain how the pneumatic can respond to the savior so readily and maturely

[10] Sagnard, Les Extraits de Théodote (Sources Chrétiennes 23), 25 f; for discussion, see Gnose (ch. 11, "La semance pneumatique") 387-415.

while the psychics cannot (CJ 13.49). I would suggest that he has made an exegetical decision to interpret the Johannine gospel in terms of the *cosmic* context, showing how it applies to the situation of those who now live in the cosmos. His exegesis of Jn 4 fulfills the *function* of the Sophia myth (which Ptolemy and Theodotus relate in pleromic and kenomic terms) : it indicates the actual process through which an alienated member of the elect discovers her "true origin" and attains gnosis. Like Ptolemy and Theodotus, Heracleon takes the doctrine of election as the theological basis of his entire exegesis.

Schottroff contests this interpretation. She claims that the myth of Sophia's redemption serves as the paradigm not of the "pneumatic elect" alone but of all who are to be saved.[11] Schottroff argues that if Sophia were the paradigm of the elect, she would be capable of liberating herself from her "passions." Nor could she truly suffer "agony," since her eventual redemption would be inevitable and certain. Yet Sophia is described in the myth as incapable of freeing herself from "pollution," and she suffers in the *kenoma* what Schottroff calls the "suspenseful" agony of her helplessness.[12]

It is clear in Heracleon's exegesis that the Samaritan (who exemplifies the experience of the archetype Sophia in the cosmos) *cannot* free herself from the conflicts she suffers. Nevertheless, she is neither "mortal" nor caught in "sins" like the psychic. Her conflict (and that of the pneumatic elect she represents) although agonizing, cannot be called "suspense" as if the outcome of her suffering were uncertain. Her pneumatic identity has been given to her *already*. As Heracleon explains, the savior "includes her as already believing, numbered among those who worship in truth" (CJ 13.16). The agony she suffers, or perhaps even her subjective illusion of suspense, arises only from her *ignorance* of that gift. What threatens her is not death, but the prolongation of her ignorance and misery before her redemption. Although she has been unaware of it, her redemption is inevitable and irresistible, as it depends not on her own efforts, but only on "the will of the Father" (CJ 13.38) in "choosing" her.

Heracleon is concerned to explicate the different "natures" so that each person may attain self-understanding, and as many psychics as possible may attain to salvation. The pneumatic will become aware of his election, and discover the reason for his dissatisfaction with merely sensual experience, and for his frustration with merely "psychic" Chris-

[11] *Glaubende,* 42-86.
[12] *Glaubende,* 64-69.

tian worship. He will discover the love of the Father who has willed to elect him, and come to worship the Father, even in the present cosmos, in "spirit and truth." The psychic, learning of the double potential intrinsic to his nature, will be encouraged to choose the way of faith and good works during his lifetime so that he may also hope for future inclusion in the ecclesia.

The development of contradictory theories concerning Valentinian anthropology becomes comprehensible when we recognize the actual complexity of their doctrine. Origen's view that Heracleon's use of generation language "proves" determinism is far oversimplified. He bases it on his own deterministic interpretation of the term *physis,* and then selects from Heracleon primarily those passages that refer to the *hylics* and *pneumatics.* He refuses to acknowledge that Heracleon describes their "generation" in language synonymous with the language of election. Schottroff bases her opposite view (that the Valentinians teach universal "free will") primarily on an examination of the passages that describe the situation of the *psychics.* As she notes, the psychics are "by nature" not elected. They stand "in the middle" between the pneumatic and hylic elements, and are bound to "choose" to identify with one or the other. But to describe the "choice" psychics make as "free will" is to apply a philosophic category that overstates the situation Heracleon describes. In attempting to use the situation of psychics as a paradigm for the salvation of all mankind, excluding election theology altogether, Schottroff fails to account for the contrary evidence: her argument appears as one-sided as Origen's.

Anti-gnostic polemics: the development of a theory of "free will"

How are we to account for the development of anti-Valentinian polemics? Langerbeck claims that the whole thrust of the polemic is based on the heresiologists' fundamental misunderstanding of gnostic anthropology. He suggests that Origen has been misled by unproven assumptions that he took from vulgarized versions of gnostic doctrine.[13] To support his theory that the Valentinians actually advocate "free will," Langerbeck is compelled to conclude that Origen spends his energy contesting a theologian who basically agrees with him on the central theological issue! How can this suggestion be reconciled with evidence that throughout the John commentary, Origen demonstrates that he has studied the text of Heracleon's commentary systematically

[13] *Aufsätze,* 69-70.

109

and in detail? On the other hand, if we recognize the doctrine of predestinarian election as the central issue at stake in the controversy, the anti-gnostic polemic becomes entirely plausible. Undeniably the heresiologists often do misinterpret Valentinian terms. But the controversy can be seen to center not on a misunderstanding, but upon a crucial theological disagreement.

The heresiologists characterize the Valentinian theory of "natures" as the teaching that some are "saved by nature" and others "lost by nature." In short, they give a polemical turn to the phrase so that, in their description, Valentinian anthropology seems to imply not *election* as its presupposition but *determinism*. Irenaeus implies this when he says that the gnostics claim to be "pneumatic by nature." This shows (he adds) their arrogance and their contempt for "good works"—"they claim to be perfect and elect" and to have "received grace as their own special possession" (AH 1.6.4).

Irenaeus, Clement, and Origen become instrumental in developing the counter-theory of *autexousia,* "free will," along with philosophic arguments for the universality of human freedom, to contradict the gnostics' alleged "determinism."

As Origen sees it, the basic issue is that of human freedom. He denies that any suggestion of predestinarian election appears in the Johannine gospel. He rejects the Valentinian practice of attributing observable differences in human spiritual insight to divine pre-election. Such differences result not from any election to grace or reprobation, but solely from each person's exercise of a wholly autonomous "free will." To sustain this theory (in view of such scriptural passages as Rom 9.10-14, where Paul describes the election of Jacob over Esau), Origen is compelled to extend this exercise of free will to the conditions of pre-existence. Quoting that passage from Paul (which the Valentinians used as a "proof text" for the doctrine of election), Origen asks:

If indeed, "when they were not yet born, and had not yet done anything, either good or evil, in order that God's election might prevail, not of works, but of him who calls," how then can it be that "there is no unrighteousness with God" when the elder serves the younger, and is hated before he has done anything that deserves slavery or hatred—unless we go back to the works done *before* this life? (CJ 2.31.)

The Valentinians also claimed that the prophecies concerning the mission and spiritual power of John the baptist, announced before his birth, give evidence of pre-election (cf Lk 1.13-15). Origen answers this by suggesting that John was not a man at all, but was actually an

110

angel who "was sent from another region when he entered into the body" (CJ 2.25). He insists in every case that the conditions of existence must result from the exercise of free will in pre-existence, so that the freedom of the creatures may retain its full integrity.

Origen even constructs his own pre-creation myth in order to refute the Valentinian myth of pre-cosmic election. He maintains that it is not the "will of God" to elect some and reject others. On the contrary, God has created all beings *equal* and *identical*. What is "given" in that original creation to "the whole rational being *(logikē ousia)* is to be in communion with the logos. This is the original situation of all human beings alike, as of all rational beings whatever (CJ Frag 45.11).

What accounts for the observable differences in human insight which the Valentinians ascribe to the "mystery" of divine election? Origen answers with the basic premise of his anthropology: every rational being effects its own changes of state through free will. The creator gives to the whole rational being the power to constitute itself through free will. The identity of each member of the rational being is located in the will.[14]

From this follows Origen's understanding of the human condition. Since identity consists in the will (which constitutes all the circumstances men experience), bodily existence itself results from such exercise of will. It expresses man's self-chosen alienation from God. The conflicts men experience in existence reflect their condition of spiritual alienation. Redemption cannot consist in the recognition of one's already given election to grace; rather redemption involves the power to reconstitute one's own being in the process of transformation toward God.

Origen's extraordinary development of the concept of *autexousia* and of his own anti-Valentinian pre-cosmic myth become comprehensible when we recognize the Valentinians among his most serious antagonists. The polemical context also may account for his virtual suppression of the doctrines of election and grace.[15]

Origen apparently considers Valentinian theology a most serious

[14] Jonas, *Gnosis*, 88 f.

[15] This helps explain why B. Drewery, in his book on *Origen and the Doctrine of Grace* (London, 1960) concludes that Origen's doctrine of grace is "a cardinal flaw" of his theology, being "infected with the disease of merit theology." According to Drewery (who apparently lacks a historical perspective on Origen's debate with the Valentinians), he "makes grace and merit so complementary as to cast an iron curtain of human capacity, human desert, and human achievement around the free grace of the Almighty . . . opening the way of the later . . . heresy of Pelagius" (205-206).

threat to his understanding of human freedom. Whether or not he actually considers them to be "determinists," he follows Clement's tactical move in shifting the ground of the debate, so that instead of directly attacking election theology, he characterizes it instead as a philosophic "determinism." Against this he marshals his arguments for "free will." If one were to adopt this philosophic framework, one would agree that Valentinian anthropology is at least partially "deterministic," but only in the sense that it presupposes divine election.

Those recent scholars who recognize the polemical bias in the charge of determinism, and who argue instead for the opposite position (that gnostic anthropology presupposes "free will") are still operating within the framework of the philosophical categories developed in antignostic polemics. Bultmann, Langerbeck, and Schottroff all discuss the Valentinian view of natures in terms of this antithesis between "determinism" and "free will." These categories neither occur in the gnostic texts themselves nor do they reflect the concerns of Valentinian theologians.

Heracleon intends the term "nature," along with the Johannine metaphors of "generation" and "seed," to interpret what he considers to be the election language of the fourth gospel. Yet his election theology is a limited one. It allows for more than the simple alternative of election to grace or reprobation. It includes a third possibility, that of "those in the middle," who, not being elected, must choose their own destiny. Schottroff points out that certain earlier gnostic literature recognizes no such third possibility. She suggests that the Valentinians may have developed this theory of the "psychic nature" in their anthropological doctrine "as a concession to the church." [16] This suggestion is appropriate to the self-consciousness of the Valentinians in relation to the emerging mainstream of the Christian church. The doctrine of the "psychic topos" enables them both to acknowledge the conversion experience of the majority of Christians as valid and effective for salvation, and to criticize it simultaneously as an incomplete apprehension of the revelation in Christ. They claim that only those who are pneumatic apprehend in the present the "true meaning" of Christ's coming, which is to reveal the Father's will in election. Yet the Valentinians recognize that those psychics who *choose* to do the Father's will in their lifetime may *also* come to gnosis at the "consummation." At that time the condemned psychics and hylics shall be destroyed, and the psychics who are saved shall be "raised" and trans-

---

[16] "Animae," 93.

formed to join in the reunion of the "whole ecclesia" with God (see above, pp. 95 f). The three designations of the "natures," then, are provisional. They express the different relations of those *in the oikonomia* to the divine election:

1) The term "psychic nature" characterizes those who are exempted from election. They stand provisionally "in the middle" between the two alternative elections of grace and reprobation, having received a capacity for attaining salvation even through their limited faith and through works.
2) The term "hylic nature" characterizes those elected to reprobation, who can also be called "lost natures."
3) The term "pneumatic nature" characterizes those who are the "elect seed," who belong to the Father who has chosen them as the elect through his will.

Synthesis: The Experiential Focus
of Valentinian Theology

By setting forth his soteriology in terms of the psychics' capacity to choose and the pneumatics' election, Heracleon criticizes the theology of "the many"—those he calls "psychic" Christians. Like other Valentinian theologians, he sees these Christians as those who unconsciously (or, to use Valentinian terminology, "ignorantly") have reified their own apprehension of the divine. They have mistaken their own apprehension of God for objective, ultimate reality. While hylics worship only what is immediately accessible to sense-perception (such as the phenomena of nature), psychics perceive this, by faith, as evidence of a being who transcends creation. They apprehend that "higher being" as the demiurge, the creator of the world and giver of the law. From the pneumatic viewpoint, however, what the psychics apprehend as their "God" is only an "image" of the higher reality—an "image" which the psychics mistakenly assume *is* the divine reality itself. For this reason, Heracleon explains, they worship the demiurge as the creator, without recognizing that the creative power of the "image" actually comes from the truly creative power (CJ 13.19). For Valentinians, the latter is described only in mythical terms, as the logos emerging from the "depth," from the "abyss," or, to use a metaphor that expresses the generative power of the "depth," from the Father.

114

Psychic worship of "the image"—the demiurge

The psychics, unaware of this, worship the *image* of God, regarding that "image" as the actual creator of the perceptible cosmos (space), the originator of its dynamic continuity (time), and the author of its ethical structure *(nomos)*. Consequently they assume that the Christian revelation comes from this "creator God," and interpret the revelation Christ offers in terms of the revelation to Israel. They assume that the revelation in Christ must be mediated, like all the activity of the demiurge, through actual events occurring in space and time. Consequently they interpret the gospels as witnesses to the historical actuality of these events, adopting historical typology as their exegetical methodology. The psychics apprehend Jesus not only, as do hylics, as a man who acts as a prophet who predicts future events, and as a thaumaturge who heals physical diseases. The psychics apprehend him as the "son of the demiurge" whose revelation conveys its inner meaning through the media of space and time.

The psychic interpretation of these events, however, is bounded not only by the epistemological structure of the creator's cosmos, but also by the ethical principles of the law he institutes. They recognize the "son of the demiurge"as also the "son of the lawgiver." The inner meaning of Christ's historically given revelation must be interpreted ethically in terms of the law. Seen from this perspective, the narrative of his healings can be interpreted ethically as the healing he offers from the "sickness of sins" through the "life-giving forgiveness." The human situation is seen as structured by the interrelation of man's physical constitution with the ethical and rational "life" breathed in him by the demiurge. Although created with free will, men have allowed themselves to fall into "sins." Thus they stand under the penalty of death. (Heracleon supports his restatement of this view by referring to Rom 1.18 f.) The savior, as "son of the demiurge," reveals himself to those who are "dying in sins" but capable of receiving life. He offers "forgiveness of sins" to all who believe in him. The sacrament of baptism, washing their physical bodies, also conveys on a psychic level that "life-giving forgiveness." Those who receive it are enabled to keep the law, so that if they willingly persevere in good works, they may attain to eternal life as their reward. So also, in their eucharist, they interpret the external physical elements of bread and wine as "signs" of an inner transformation. Recalling the passion and death of Jesus, they regard these as the means of "forgiveness," and eschatologically as an anticipation of the "age to come."

The psychics anticipate that the dualistic structure of their present experience is to be overcome eschatologically, the pneumatic component to be transformed, and the psychic component to be resolved into an eternal harmony with the creator. In the present age, however, the psychics understand their experience of revelation in terms of their freedom to choose the works that lead to "death for sins," or to repent and choose instead to accept forgiveness, and turn to the works of "eternal life."

Historians may realize that this Valentinian description of the psychic topos offers a fully recognizable description of the emerging mainstream of Christians in the second century as it is known from other historical and literary sources. As the Valentinian description of "the many" is clearly biased and polemically constructed, the historian may criticize this description as one-sided, as the theologian may dispute its theological premises. One may suggest, however, that this description of "the many" is at least no more biased than the heresiologist's descriptions of the Valentinians. It may be even less so, for while the heresiologists reject Valentinian theology as totally false, the Valentinians (unlike many other gnostic groups) do not wholly reject what they call the "psychic" interpretation of the revelation. In common with all Christians, they do reject (as hylic) any interpretation of Christ that is limited to sense-perception of him alone. The Valentinians acknowledge, however, the validity of the psychic apprehension in its own terms.

They also insist that the psychic "standpoint" offers a radically limited perspective. Those who stand at that level, they claim, have no possibility of attaining to the third and higher level of insight. Since their perception is structured according to the mode of rational reflection on sense-experience, the psychics can perceive "God" only in these terms, as the creator of the world and active agent in history. Their standpoint offers no possibility of recognizing that their "creator god" is not in himself an absolute reality, that the "creator" they apprehend is only an "image" (CJ 13.19; Exc 47.2-3; AH 1.5.2). The Valentinians understand this "image" in a non-absolutistic sense as a sign that points toward reality. The whole of "psychic" theology, indeed, of all theological language, in their view, consists of a series of such "images." Insofar as these "images" become reified and absolutized, as they do for those at the psychic level, they function demonically: they hinder the development of spiritual insight.

The Valentinians describe this process of reification mythically in terms of the demiurge's "ignorance." The demiurge, created as an "image" and "likeness" of the higher powers, himself is ignorant of those powers of which his own existence is an expression. He imagines that he himself is the only absolute and autonomous creative power; he "imagines that he himself is all things." He acts as if he were wholly autonomous, claiming that he alone "is God, and there is none other" (AH 1.5.3).

Certain gnostic theologians evaluate the demiurge's self-assertion in a wholly negative way. They describe him as hostile to those who seek higher insight (*gnōsis*). According to this view, the "images" of God only hinder the process of attaining spiritual insight. The Valentinians, however, see that the apparent autonomy of the image has a special function to fulfill in the process of redemption.[1] Naïve reification may, in their view, serve as a stage in the process of attaining insight. This is expressed in the myth of the demiurge's "conversion." For when the savior (the logos) reveals himself as emerging from that higher creative power, the demiurge gives up his own naïve and absolutistic stance, acknowledging his own ignorance. He confesses, in Heracleon's words, that he himself is "lesser than" Christ (see Jn 1.26-30). He recognizes Christ, with humility and joy, as coming from that higher creative power from which he himself has emerged (CJ 6.39).

Those who remain at the psychic level, however, are those who persist in reifying the "image" as absolute in itself. In Heracleon's words, they take the "images" to be the reality. They fall into the error described by Paul in Rom 1.25 of worshiping the "creation and not the creator." Those at the pneumatic level, however, rightly recognize the demiurge as an "image" of God, a sign of the "true creator," which is Christ, or the logos (as Heracleon explains with a reference to Jn 1.3). From the pneumatic viewpoint, insofar as such "images" are reified, they hinder the believer from attaining true understanding, and keep him "in flesh and error." Whoever comes to understand these *as images* does not deny their validity, but does relativize it. Such a person alone realizes what the "images" signify when interpreted "in spirit and in truth" (CJ 13.19). To realize this is to

---

[1] AH 1.5.3: "They say that the demiurge thought he had created these things himself (ἀφ' ἑαυτοῦ) and therefore they say he was ignorant of the forms (τὰς ἰδέας) of the things he made, and of the Mother herself. He thought that he alone was 'all things.' They say that the reason for this having happened to him is the Mother's own doing, that she intended to bring him forth in this way, as head and source of his own being, and ruler of his own being, and ruler of his entire activity (κεφαλὴν μὲν καὶ ἀρχὴν τῆς ἰδίας οὐσίας, κύριον δὲ τῆς ὅλης πραγματείας)."

experience the transformation onto a higher level of consciousness. It is to be transformed from the psychic to the pneumatic topos.

Psychic salvation and gospel history

The psychics' error, however, is not only that they reify the "image" of the creator. In the same way they also reify the figure of Jesus Christ and the events narrated of him in, for example, the fourth gospel. The Valentinians see the same error involved in psychic exegesis. The Valentinians, of course, in common with all Christians, agree that the gospel cannot be read *as revelation* so long as it is read only literally. Literal (or in their terms, "hylic") exegesis, would read it simply as the historical account of the words and deeds of Jesus of Nazareth. But, the Valentinians add, in distinction from "the majority," neither is the gospel to be interpreted only "psychically," that is, as revelation actually given *in* and *through* historical events. Such a reading, in their view, reifies and absolutizes the *events themselves* as being the actual revelation of the demiurge given "in history." What the psychics fail to apprehend is that the events of the oikonomia, such as Jesus' birth and death, are themselves "images." Psychic Christians, reifying these, insist that salvation comes to them only *because* these events actually occurred, only because the son of the demiurge actually entered into human history. They fail to realize that these events can only be understood "spiritually" as signs and symbols of a spiritual process that is not bound to specific time and place.

This does not mean that the Valentinians deny the historical actuality of the events narrated in John. On the contrary, Heracleon apparently assumes that the events *did* happen historically. Yet their historical actuality remains irrelevant and meaningless apart from the higher levels of exegesis. Indeed, the "hylic level" of historical narration can be worse than irrelevant. Improperly understood, it can serve as an obstacle to understanding, since its historical form allows the possibility of reading the account on the historical level alone, and thus reading it in "error and ignorance."

The psychics, although they are not literalists, nevertheless consider the historical actuality of the events to be the criterion of the validity of their preaching. So Justin, for example, warns against reading the gospels except as witnesses to the events themselves. The Valentinians insist, on the contrary, that only when all the objects, events, and persons described in John are interpreted as "images of things in the

118

pleroma," that is, as symbols of a reality that transcends space, time, and nomos, is the gospel read "in spirit and in truth." Only by such an exegetical process does the written account *become* revelation for the reader.

Pneumatic worship of the Father of Truth

It is for this reason that the Valentinians reject the exegetical methodology of "the many" and develop instead an exegetical discipline that presupposes the symbolic (pneumatic) level of apprehension. For Heracleon, the primary task of such exegesis is to distinguish the three levels in the account, and then to interpret the whole "pneumatically," that is, symbolically.

If the events of Christ's coming are only "images" of a higher reality, and if the demiurge is only the "creation" and "image" of a higher creative power, one must ask the obvious questions: what is that creative power which "creates" these "images"? What is the "reality" to which the "images" refer?

The Valentinians insist that the reality which the pneumatics apprehend is essentially indescribable and ineffable. They call it the "depth," the "abyss," the "Father." [2] Even to use these metaphors is to acknowledge, however, that insofar as one can refer to that ineffable being, one's expression takes the indirect form of "images." So the logos, who mediates between the Father and other beings, himself is only an "image" of the Father. The Valentinians, then far from intending to do away with "images," understand "images" and symbols as the *only* means of pointing to or signifying a reality which is essentially ineffable. The primary act of insight (*gnōsis*) is to recognize that all figures of religious tradition *are* images and not themselves the "reality" that is being signified. The Valentinian theologian, therefore, concerns himself with the "images" given in the gospels and the apostolic writings to show how these indicate and signify what is beyond them. They themselves characteristically express the higher levels of apprehension, the "mysteries of gnosis," in mythical and symbolic language. For that "reality" is not given to human experience, in their

---

[2] See discussion in Puech-Quispel, "Quatrième Ecrit," 71 f; Sagnard, *Gnose*, 296-299, 325-333, 487; AH 1.1.1: "They say there exists in the invisible and ineffable heights above a perfect, pre-existent aion (τέλειον αἰῶνα προόντα) which they call primal Arche, primal Father, Abyss (προαρχὴν καὶ προπάτορα καὶ βυθὸν). Incomprehensible and invisible, eternal and unengendered, he remained throughout innumerable cycles of ages in profound repose and quiescence."

view, *either* in immediate sense-perception, *or* in rational and ethical reflection on such perception.

Pneumatic redemption as recognition of election

But Heracleon's primary concern is neither to expound these epistemological principles nor to reiterate the virtual impossibility of directly apprehending the divine. His concern instead is to show what the pneumatic apprehension means in the experience of redemption.

The psychic level of apprehension offers no possibility for interpreting the experience of conversion except in terms of ethical choice and action.

Heracleon never claims that the psychic experience of conversion is false or invalid. On the contrary, he agrees that those who undergo such conversion (like the ruler's son of Jn 4) may attain "eternal life." He does see the psychic view of conversion, however, as radically limited. Being structured according to rational and ethical modes of thought, the pyschic view of the conversion experience is limited to these categories.

The Valentinians, on the other hand, claim to apprehend the experience of their redemption on a level that can neither be limited to the psychic standpoint nor comprehended in its terms. As we have seen, Heracleon recognizes the Samaritan as the paradigm of the pneumatic conversion. Those who share in this paradigm, having participated in the doctrine and worship of the "majority," have become frustrated and dissatisfied with it. When they hear the offer of "living water" they realize at once that the Christian worship in which they have shared cannot offer it. They come to perceive the whole psychic paradigm as inadequate for them. They do not experience themselves as those who, having heard the preaching, are "called" to "repent of their sins" and to receive forgiveness in order to turn to good works with new resolution. They encounter the revelation in Christ as a recognition of their own hidden, unknown, true identity, an identity that they realize cannot be worked for or gained by their own effort, but is "given" freely to them. Their experience cannot be described, either, as an act of their own choice or decision. On the contrary, they experience the awareness of already having been "chosen" (CJ 13.16). Their response to the savior is not one of crisis and decision, but of immediate, uncritical, spontaneous faith (CJ 13.10).

In the overwhelming sense of divine grace given to them, they are untroubled by a sense of guilt over their sins. They recall their former lives with bewilderment and shame at their former ignorance of God and of their own needs. Their concern, however, is not to be "forgiven," but to find a way of accounting for their former ignorance and alienation (CJ 13.15).

Valentinian theology, like Heracleon's exegesis of Jn 4.21 f, attempts to explicate the difference between the three different "levels" of worship. Through it the pneumatics come to realize that they have been living in alienation from themselves and from God on lower levels of awareness (hylic and psychic) which are alien to their own inner being. They now learn to recognize how all the terms of psychic worship bear higher, symbolic meaning. They apprehend their own affinity with the Father as those whom he "wills to save" (CJ 13.38) and has chosen already as "his own" (CJ 13.20). But they experience their redemption as having nothing to do with their own will, or free choice, or works. It is offered them freely as the "grace and gift of the savior" that depends on the Father's will alone, and therefore can never be taken away or destroyed (CJ 13.10).

Receiving this recognition, they now realize that they are to go and preach "the presence of Christ" to the psychics, in order to bring them to the savior, where each may encounter him according to his own capacity (CJ 13.31). The psychic may, through this evangelizing, be "called" to repentance and faith, and attain "eternal life." The pneumatic who still is unaware of his true identity may come thereby to recognize himself as one of the "chosen."

Heracleon claims that Jn 4 demonstrates how the process of conversion occurs on two qualitatively different levels of insight and experience. The Valentinian theory of different "levels" enables him to differentiate these without having to reject either one as false. He is able to sustain, for example, the validity of the psychic level, while simultaneously showing how it is limited and bounded to ethical categories. He also is able to point beyond the psychic to that level incomprehensible in its terms—to the experience of redemption as the elect receive it.

The Valentinians, I would argue, are concerned primarily to express their apprehension of the experience of redemption on this level. In doing so they claim to present no new doctrine or theory, but only to expound the theology of election and grace they claim to find especially in the writings of Paul and John. In the majority of Christian groups around them, however, they find that the preaching consists predominately of a moralizing paraenesis. Human freedom and responsibility for ethical decision and action are stressed by many Christian apologists contemporary with them, above all to counter the fatalism of pagan religion and philosophy. It is not only Christians, of course, who stress the human capacity of self-constitution (*autexousia*) against fatalism, and who are ready to dismiss this election theology as determinism, if not as "arrogance." Plotinus, for example, castigates the Valentinians for precisely these reasons and indicts them for failing to produce any ethical treatises! [3]

The Valentinians, however, do not wholly deny the efficacy of human will and human choice, at least in the case of the "many." They deny it only in the case of the elect, whose redemption is comprehensible to them solely in terms of the *divine* will and choice. Their position of asserting this "pneumatic" theology against that of the majority, and of attempting to sustain both psychic and pneumatic theology as valid on different levels, has impelled the Valentinians to develop their theology in two directions. First, it has impelled them to express their apprehension of election in mythical and symbolic terms; secondly, to develop a theoretical understanding of religious language as (in their view) necessarily imagistic and symbolic.

---

[3] *Ennead* 2.9.15 (in: *Plotinus: Psychic and Ethical Treatises, Enn. 2 and 3:* transl. and ed. S. MacKenna [London, 1921], 237): "This school, in fact, is convicted by its neglect of any mention of virtue. Any discussion of such (ethical) matters is missing entirely. We are not told what virtue is, or under what different kinds it appears; there is no word of all the numerous and noble reflections on it that have come down to us from the ancients; we do not learn what constitutes it, or how it is acquired; how the soul is tended, or how it is purified. For them to say 'look to God' is not very helpful without some instruction as to what this means . . . in terms of right conduct."

Glossary-Index of Technical Greek Terms

aion
member of pleroma, 24-27, 32-33,
37, 76-77
revealed in cosmos by syzygos, 74,
76-77
revealed in kenoma by savior, 37
totality of pleroma, 48, 62
transformation-state of ecclesia, 96

anthropos
body of Christ, 69-70
heavenly Adam, 20-21
inner anthropos, 79
pleromic syzygos of Ecclesia, 33, 93
pneumatic elect, 33-35, 90, 93
primal anthropos, 20-21
syzygos of Zoe, 37

apolytrosis
"bridechamber," 78-82, 91-92
contrasted with baptism, 60-65
"passover," 76-78
reception of gnosis, 91-92
sacramental formulae, 62-64, 78-82
Valentinian sacrament, 62-65, 78-82

arche
arche of "the whole," 26-27
Father (Clement), 38
great arche, 23
primal arche, 21
son, monogenes, theos, 26-27, 42

cosmos
creation of, 28-34, 47-48
eidetic (formal), 22-23, 67
psychics as *cosmos,* 93-94
savior's entry into, 33-34, 74-78,
93-94
unbegotten/self - generated/formal,
22-23

demiurge
"Abraham," 87, 100, 101
"creation" of logos, 75, 89-90, 114,
117
creator of cosmos, 30-31, 106, 107
creator of materiality, 21-23
his "conversion," 52-56, 116-18

demiurge—cont'd
"image" of the Father, 90, 114-18
"Jacob," 86-87
"John the baptist," 52-64
lawgiver/judge, 29, 62, 86-87
"Moses," 86-87

ecclesia
emergence in cosmos, 33, 35, 90-92
pleromic syzygos of Anthropos, 32-
35, 41, 70, 93
pneumatic ecclesia, 68-82
"Samaritan woman," 77-78, 86-97
"temple," 68-82
totality of "the called" and "elect,"
95-97

gnosis
"initiation into gnosis," 4-16, 20-21,
26-27, 41-43, 61, 65
perceived pneumatically, 52-66
recognition of election, 77, 79, 90-
92, 107-13
recognition of "truth," 82, 90-93,
119-20

hylic
"Capernaum," 52, 67, 85
characterized by ignorance, 54-57,
59, 89, 114
"error and falsehood," 100-104, 118
generated from devil, 100-104
hylic *nature:* pre-elected, 100-104,
113
hylic *topos:* materiality, 52, 56-57,
67, 89
"Mt. Gezirim," 89

hypothesis
of "orthodox" faith, 11, 43
of Valentinian theology, 43, 48-49

kenoma
second state of creation, 24-28, 33-
35, 37
void, 24

logos
creator/savior in cosmos, 30-38, 47-
48, 114, 117

123

Index of Biblical Passages and Other References

Index of Persons and Subjects

(Numbers in italics refer to footnote numbers)